the way to go home

KV-419-149

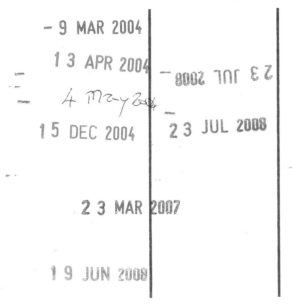
habilitation

ommented on the need for better rehabilitation
he Government.

of Rehabilitation Services

of services is needed that includes inpatient
ediate care and community services.

Rehabilitation Programme

a clear care pathway, which requires

Rehabilitation Services

an be increased by using therapy assistants
herapists more flexibly.

trategic Approach

requires a shared understanding of what is
-systems approach.

E7G78

Contents

Preface	3

1 The Role of Rehabilitation — 4

Introduction	5
The growing interest in rehabilitation services for older people	5
What is rehabilitation?	7
What form should rehabilitation take?	8
Who needs rehabilitation?	9
How should rehabilitation be organised?	10

2 The Provision of Rehabilitation Services — 12

Measuring the provision of rehabilitation services	13
Inpatient rehabilitation	14
Intermediate rehabilitation services	21
Day and community-based services	30
Linking services	39
Conclusion	43
Recommendations	44

3 Managing the Rehabilitation Programme — 45

Care pathways	46
Organising and delivering care	56
Conclusion	63
Recommendations	64

4 Therapists and Rehabilitation Services — 65

Maximising the use of skills	74
Improving flexibility	80
Recommendations	83

5 Developing A Strategic Approach — 84

A shared understanding	85
The use of new 'financial flexibilities'	91
The cost effectiveness of rehabilitation	93
Conclusion	94
Recommendations	95

Appendix 1	96
External advisory group	

Appendix 2	97
Stroke	

Appendix 3	100
The role of therapists	

References	103
Index	107

© Audit Commission 2000

First published in June 2000 by the Audit Commission for Local Authorities and the National Health Service in England and Wales, 1 Vincent Square, London SW1P 2PN

Printed in the UK for the Audit Commission by Belmont Press, Northampton

ISBN 1 86240 221 3

Photographs: Judy Harrison/Format (p65), Sandra Lousada/Collections (p38), David Mansell (pp9, 25, 45, 58, 84), Brenda Prince/Format (cover, p12), Hilary Shedel (pp3, 49), Sam Tanner/Photofusion (pp4, 27)

Preface

The Audit Commission oversees the external audit of local authorities and the National Health Service (NHS) in England and Wales. As part of this function, the Commission is required to undertake studies to enable it to make recommendations for improving the economy, efficiency and effectiveness of services provided by these bodies.

Over the last two years, the Commission has been reviewing rehabilitation services for older people, and its findings are set out in this report. Cross-cutting audits of these services, covering health and social care, will take place throughout England and Wales during 2000 and 2001. For the first time, a single auditor has been appointed to work with all health and social care agencies within local areas.

This is the fourth in a series of reports with the common theme of promoting independence for older people. The other reports in the series have looked at services for older people with mental health problems (*Forget Me Not* (Ref. 1)), the provision of disability equipment to older or disabled people (*Fully Equipped* (Ref. 2)) and charging arrangements for home care by local authorities (*Charging with Care* (Ref. 3)). It follows a previous report *The Coming of Age* (Ref. 4) published in 1997, which reviewed the health and social care of older people.

In the course of the study, fieldwork has been carried out in 12 areas of England and Wales, with visits to health trusts (acute and community), health authorities and local authority social services. In a few of these areas completely different services were provided in different parts, so that they functioned independently, providing information on up to 16 different sets of services. In the report these data are referred to as 'Audit Commission study site data'.

The Audit Commission has also carried out a data collection exercise collecting information by authority and trust, and collating some of this information by locality. This report presents the first analysis of these data. These data are referred to as 'Audit Commission locality data' in the report.

The study on which this report is based was carried out by Stuart Turnock, Chris Baker and Maggie Kemmner under the direction of David Browning. Data preparation and analysis was carried out by Louise Cloke, Justin Caldwell and Tom Dixon. Particular thanks go to all of our study sites and to Dr Michael Whitelaw and Mary Crawford, professional advisers to the study. Thanks also go to our external advisory group, listed at Appendix 1; and to John Pears of District Audit and Phil Blake who have played a major part in shaping the audit.

1

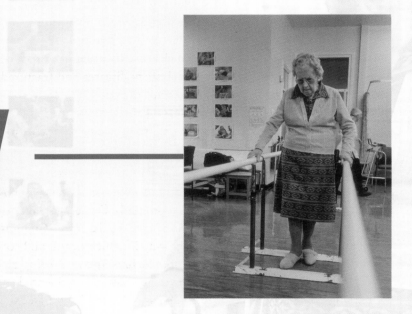

The Role of Rehabilitation

Many people have commented on the need for better rehabilitation services, and their comments have been endorsed by government policy. But effective rehabilitation is complex, requiring a range of services, clear care pathways and good organisation.

Introduction

1.   Older people are major users of health and social services. Nationally, those aged over 65 make up 16 per cent of the population, but account for nearly one-half of Department of Health (DoH) expenditure and local authority social services expenditure (Ref. 4). The proportion of the total population aged over 65 is set to grow in the coming decades, with three times as many people over 85 estimated by 2050 (Ref. 5). These 'very old' people are particularly high users of acute hospitals and other health and social services.

The growing interest in rehabilitation services for older people

2.   Older people tend to suffer from chronic disease and disability: conditions such as stroke, cardio-respiratory diseases and fractured neck of femur all become more common as people age (Ref. 6). They are more likely to benefit from multidisciplinary assessment and rehabilitation. They are also likely to require more time than younger patients to make a full recovery.

3.   The Audit Commission's 1995 report *United They Stand* (Ref. 7), on the care of people with fractured neck of femur, found that few hospitals organised rehabilitation services well, especially for people who needed more time. In *The Coming of Age* (1997) (Ref. 4), the Audit Commission drew attention to shortcomings in the way in which health and social services worked together to improve procedures and to develop services that would offer alternatives to unnecessary hospital, residential care or nursing home admission. The Commission found health and social services locked in a vicious circle **[EXHIBIT 1, overleaf]**. Rising hospital admissions and falling lengths of stay were reducing time for recovery and rehabilitation, and leading to increasing (and unsustainable) demands on social services, especially for residential and nursing home placements. These demands were absorbing resources, reducing funds for community services that could have helped to contain rising hospital admissions.

4.   A number of other agencies and bodies have commented on the potential of rehabilitation services – including the DoH, NHS Executive, Social Services Inspectorate (SSI), House of Commons Health Select Committee, Royal Commission on Long Term Care, British Geriatric Society and the King's Fund.

5.   From Government, the comments have been backed by policy statements – in England in the DoH's executive letter *Better Services For Vulnerable People* (BSVP) (Ref. 8) published in October 1997. This required health and local authorities to develop rehabilitation services, to improve assessment arrangements and to create joint investment plans (JIPs). A further circular followed – *Better Services For Vulnerable People – Maintaining the Momentum* (Ref. 9) – which stressed the links between the BSVP agenda and other agendas and national priorities. It emphasised the contribution that rehabilitation can make to the management of demand across the health and social care economy. Authorities were guided to ensure that:

- procedures are in place to help them to identify those older people in hospital who are more likely to benefit from focused rehabilitation;

- services are in place that give older people time to recuperate, and enable professionals to work with them on rounded assessments and care plans;

- rehabilitation services, in a variety of settings, are in place to help older people in hospital regain optimum levels of independence and to return home; and

- community-based services are reviewed to help prevent hospital admissions of older people.

In Wales, guidance has stressed the importance of multi-agency planning and there is a high expectation that health authorities and local authorities will work together.

EXHIBIT 1

The vicious circle

Health and social services are locked into a vicious circle.

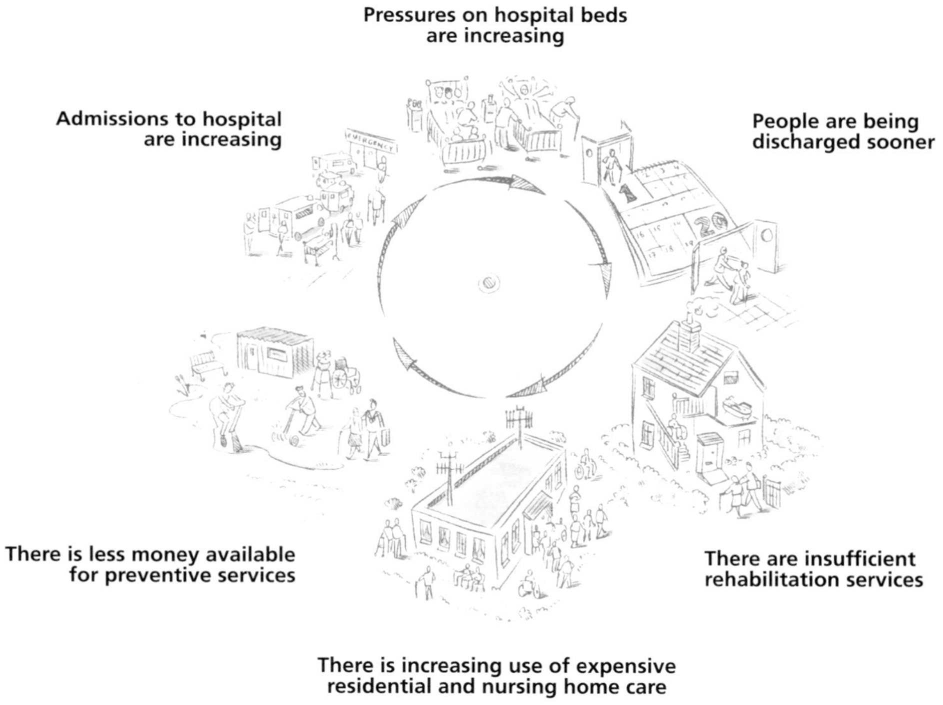

Pressures on hospital beds are increasing

Admissions to hospital are increasing

People are being discharged sooner

There is less money available for preventive services

There are insufficient rehabilitation services

There is increasing use of expensive residential and nursing home care

Source: Audit Commission

...rehabilitation will usually require a mixture of clinical, therapeutic and social interventions...

6. Arrangements that allow closer joint working are also being strengthened following the consultation papers *Partnership in Action* (Ref. 10) in England and *Partnership for Improvement* (Ref. 11) in Wales. These papers and subsequent guidance, set out the basis for new flexibilities for funding health and social care to help the development of the integrated services required for good rehabilitation. The *NHS Act 1999* (Ref. 12) now allows pooled funds, lead commissioning and integrated services.

7. In England, the BSVP initiative has been reinforced by other guidance, including *Modernising Health and Social Services: National Priorities Guidance 1999/2000–2001/02* (Ref. 13). In Wales, the *Better Wales* (Ref. 14) consultation paper is proposing to 'help the elderly and those with disabilities to live independently, and support their carers'.

8. The White Paper *Modernising Social Services* (Ref. 15), published in November 1998, required adult social services to help to promote older people's independence by 'providing the support needed by someone to make the most of their own capacity and potential'. This paper has been supported by additional resources between 1999 and 2002 in the form of three specific grants: the Partnership Grant, the Carers' Grant and the Prevention Grant. Together they provide £747 million.

9. In 2000, a National Service Framework (NSF) for older people is due to be published. The framework is intended to improve the quality of care services and to decrease inequities in health services for older people across the country.

What is rehabilitation?

10. A review of *Trends in Rehabilitation Policy* (Ref. 16), commissioned jointly by the Audit Commission and the King's Fund, concluded that 'there is widespread confusion about the meaning of rehabilitation, making it difficult at times to distinguish it from other forms of care and support'. This review observed that rehabilitation is 'often a function of services, not necessarily a service in its own right'. It recognised that while the literature contains a range of ideas and definitions of rehabilitation, there is an emerging consensus that:

- the primary objective of rehabilitation involves restoration to the maximum degree possible, either of function (physical or mental) or role (within the family, social network or workforce);
- rehabilitation usually requires a mixture of clinical, therapeutic and social interventions that also address issues relevant to a person's physical and social environment; and
- effective rehabilitation needs to be responsive to users' needs and wishes, to be purposeful, involve a number of agencies and disciplines and be available when required.

What form should rehabilitation take?

11. A second review, *Effective Practice in Rehabilitation* (Ref. 17) commissioned jointly by the Audit Commission and the King's Fund, found that although there are gaps in the evidence base, there 'are positive results for the effectiveness of rehabilitation in a variety of key areas'. The 'effect sizes that have been shown in these positive reviews are very large and exceed many of those seen with drug treatments'. Four key themes run through the evidence – the need for access, assessment, organisation and continuity.

Access

12. Access to rehabilitation needs to be available when required – through appropriate arrangements for assessment and to appropriate services in a range of settings.

Assessment

13. There is strong evidence that comprehensive assessment, followed by the implementation of individual care plans, reduces the risk of older people being re-admitted to hospitals or placed in long-stay care. It also improves survival rates and physical and cognitive functioning.

Organisation

14. The appropriate organisation of services is also critical to their effectiveness. Services should 'be organised to achieve co-ordination of different interventions and different phases of the rehabilitation process'. Furthermore, the 'more one can achieve co-ordination of diverse inputs through a systematic approach, protocol or team delivery, the more effective the rehabilitation may be'. The evidence here is particularly strong for stroke care, where there is co-ordinated multidisciplinary care, education, training and the specialisation of staff.

Continuity

15. Finally, continuity of care is essential. Where people receiving rehabilitation are transferred between different services, it is essential that their care plan is transferred with them. Services 'should be organised to achieve co-ordination of different interventions and different phases of the rehabilitative process'. However, managing and delivering this complexity in practice is difficult. It requires a multiplicity of agencies, professions and services to work together, even though they are all funded, managed and held accountable through different means.

Who needs rehabilitation?

16. Everyone who has had an illness or accident needs some time to recover. Most, especially younger people, do not need much help to regain their fitness and take up their lives where they left off. But some, especially older people, need more help, and some will need constant help. Each older person needs an individual response but, broadly speaking, people recovering can be divided into three groups:

- Those who will recover quickly and who do not need more than a limited amount of help with rehabilitation.

- Those who will take much more time and who need a lot more help.

- Those whose recovery will be limited, and who will need palliative or continuing care.

17. The vicious circle [**EXHIBIT 1, p6**] occurs where members of the second group are treated as if they belonged to the third group. This report focuses on the needs of people in the second group who are aged 75 and over, and looks at how rehabilitation can best be provided for them.

18. Older people who need rehabilitation suffer from a wide range of conditions. Many – perhaps most – suffer from more than one condition. Their needs are often complex. The Royal College of Physicians explains that:

'Focal disease may have a global impact in a biologically aged patient such that a common and familiar acute condition may present in atypical fashion. An elderly patient with pneumonia may present with the effects of cerebral hypoxia and toxaemia, confusion, impaired mobility and urinary incontinence. The presentation may seem rather unfavourable, with a reversible underlying problem presenting as an apparently irreversible general breakdown. The presence of other concurrent diseases increases the chance of a particular condition leading to dependency and loss of function: so-called "multiple pathology".' (Ref. 18)

This, often together with poor economic, social and environmental support, means that the circumstances of older people are often very complex, and illness is frequently associated with acute or chronic disability.

19. To provide some focus, this study has looked at the rehabilitation of people whose primary condition is stroke as a 'tracer condition'. Stroke has been chosen for a number of reasons. Firstly, it is very prevalent. It is the third most common cause of death in the UK after all cancers and coronary heart disease, and accounts for about one in ten of all deaths. Some 88 per cent of stroke deaths are in people over 65 (Ref. 19). Stroke is also the leading cause of major disability and handicap in the UK, with 35 per cent of survivors still functionally dependent after one year [**APPENDIX 2, PART A**]. It therefore places a major burden on families and health and social services.

20. Secondly, it is relatively easy to identify and it is recorded using the international classification of diseases (ICD) so that it is possible to use the group of people who have suffered from a stroke as a sampling frame. A survey of such people has been carried out to get their views on the rehabilitation they received [APPENDIX 2, PART B].

21. Thirdly, as reported above, the evidence for the benefits of organised stroke care, including rehabilitation, is now very well established. Patients managed by a specialist co-ordinated stroke team in a stroke unit have lower mortality and morbidity rates and these benefits are achieved at no more cost than managing patients in non-specialist wards and units, according to the Stroke Unit Trialists' Collaboration (Ref. 20). They have reported a 23 per cent reduction in death, with 60 deaths prevented per 1,000 patients treated.

22. Fourthly, the principles that apply to stroke care can be applied more widely. *Effective Practice in Rehabilitation* (Ref. 17) recommended that 'stroke care may be an appropriate model for understanding the efficacy of rehabilitation in other situations' where several disciplines have a distinctive and complementary role to play and where several inputs need to be co-ordinated. It recommends that the evidence (together with that for assessment) should 'be translated into routine practice and used to inform rehabilitation developments for other conditions'.

How should rehabilitation be organised?

23. The organisation of rehabilitation should match the needs of the people likely to benefit from it. These needs are many and various. However, building on the research described above, a number of broad principles can be set out.

24. A range of services is needed to provide good access to rehabilitation. For people admitted to hospital, rehabilitation starts as part of their acute care. For those who require more time, it may continue on specialist rehabilitation wards, where they remain under the supervision of specialist medical and nursing staff as part of an intensive multidisciplinary rehabilitation programme. Over time, the need for clinical supervision reduces as their medical problems are stabilised, but they may still need help to recover and rebuild their confidence. The need for more intensive therapy support increases, while the need for medical and nursing care reduces, and 'intermediate care' between hospital and home may be appropriate. Finally, people at home or who have returned home after hospital, may need access to specialist assessment and rehabilitation from a multidisciplinary team operating in the community. Four main service types are therefore relevant [EXHIBIT 2]. These are discussed in Chapter 2.

25. People need to follow a clear care pathway while receiving rehabilitation. Arrangements need to be in place to screen people to pick up those who need rehabilitation – whether they are at home or on acute hospital wards. Thorough multidisciplinary assessment is then needed, followed by clear care plans and arrangements for delivering care.

EXHIBIT 2

Rehabilitation services

Four main service types are relevant.

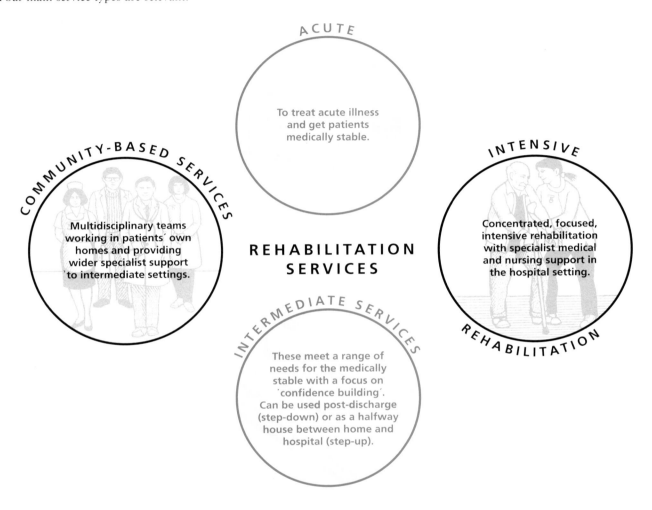

ACUTE
To treat acute illness and get patients medically stable.

COMMUNITY-BASED SERVICES
Multidisciplinary teams working in patients' own homes and providing wider specialist support to intermediate settings.

INTENSIVE
Concentrated, focused, intensive rehabilitation with specialist medical and nursing support in the hospital setting.
REHABILITATION

REHABILITATION SERVICES

INTERMEDIATE SERVICES
These meet a range of needs for the medically stable with a focus on 'confidence building'. Can be used post-discharge (step-down) or as a halfway house between home and hospital (step-up).

Source: Audit Commission

Arrangements are also needed to ensure that rehabilitation programmes continue when people move to another location. All of these arrangements call for good co-ordination and multidisciplinary working, as described in Chapter 3. Therapists are key members of any multidisciplinary team – particularly occupational, speech and language and physiotherapists – and this report considers in some detail in Chapter 4 and Appendix 3 how their contribution is being managed. Finally, all of these various contributions need to be brought together within a plan for delivering better rehabilitation services that makes full use of new policies and opportunities, as described in Chapter 5.

2

The Provision of Rehabilitation Services

A range of services is needed. In hospital, rehabilitation starts with acute care, but for those who require more time, it may continue on specialist rehabilitation wards and in intermediate care. People at home, or returned home, need the support of a multidisciplinary re-ablement team.

31. The amount of therapy available per bed sometimes contrasts with the number of beds available [**EXHIBIT 6**]. This raises the issue of whether some beds are labelled 'rehabilitation', but are used in different ways. For example:

- Authority K appears to have high numbers of rehabilitation beds, but it provides low levels of therapy per bed day.
- Authority C appears to have low numbers of rehabilitation beds, but it provides high levels of therapy per bed day.

The wards with low levels of therapy are not well placed to provide active rehabilitation. Authorities and trusts need to be sure that they are clear about what they are trying to achieve with beds provided for the rehabilitation of older people.

EXHIBIT 6

Qualified therapy time per bed compared to numbers of rehabilitation beds

The amount of therapy available per bed sometimes contrasts with the number of beds available.

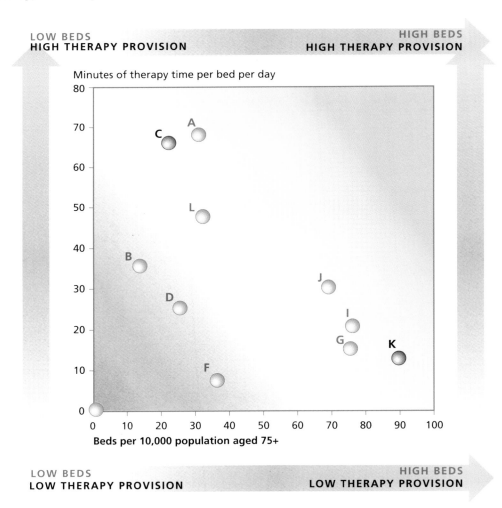

Source: Audit Commission study site data

Stroke units

32. Rehabilitation for people who have suffered a stroke is best organised on separate stroke units, although 7 of the 16 sites visited did not have them [EXHIBIT 7], and in 1 case that did, there were only 5 beds. Therapy input per bed was consistently high in the five units in which full data were collected [EXHIBIT 8].

EXHIBIT 7

Study site provision

All had inpatient rehabilitation beds, but not all provided organised stroke rehabilitation through stroke units.

SITES	1	2	3	4	5	6	7	8	9	10	11	12	13	14	15	16
REHABILITATION BEDS	✓	✓	✓	✓	✓	✓	✓	✓	✓	✓	✓ COMB	✓ COMB	✓ COMB	✓	✓	✓
STROKE UNITS	✓	✓	✓	✓	✓	✓	✓	✓	✓	✗	✗	✗	✗	✗	✗	✗

Note: COMB refers only to sites with combined acute and rehabilitation wards.

Source: Audit Commission study site data

EXHIBIT 8

Qualified therapy time: available minutes per bed per day for occupational therapy, physiotherapy and speech and language therapy in stroke units

Input was consistently high in the five units in which full data were collected.

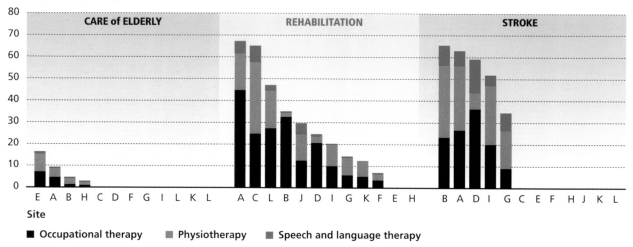

Minutes per bed per day

■ Occupational therapy ■ Physiotherapy ■ Speech and language therapy

Source: Audit Commission study site data

33. A further sample from a different set of localities (Audit Commission locality data – see Preface) found stroke units in under three-quarters of them, and the number of beds available for rehabilitation varying by a factor of five [**EXHIBIT 9**].

EXHIBIT 9

Stroke units

The number of beds available for rehabilitation varied by a factor of five.

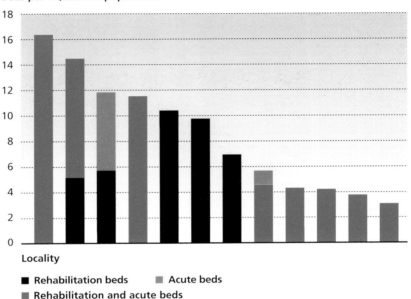

Beds per 10,000 75+ population

Locality

■ Rehabilitation beds   ■ Acute beds
■ Rehabilitation and acute beds

Source: Audit Commission locality data collection

34. However, many stroke units concentrated on younger people [**EXHIBIT 10**]. Admissions of people aged 75 or over per head of population varied widely [**EXHIBIT 11**]. There is nothing in the evidence that suggests that older people should be excluded from organised stroke care.

EXHIBIT 10

Proportion of stroke unit admissions aged 75 or over

Many units concentrated on younger people.

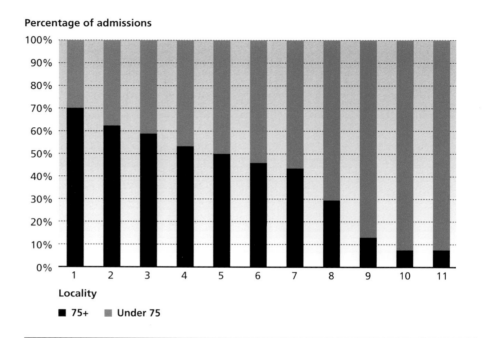

Percentage of admissions

Locality

■ 75+   ■ Under 75

Source: Audit Commission locality data collection

EXHIBIT 11

Stroke unit admissions

Admissions of those aged 75 or over varied widely.

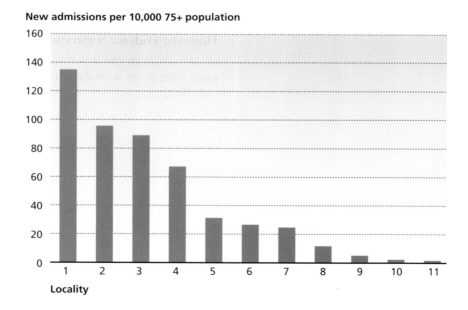

New admissions per 10,000 75+ population

Locality

Source: Audit Commission locality data collection

Intermediate rehabilitation services

35. Some areas appear to rely entirely on hospitals to provide rehabilitation. But once people's medical condition has stabilised, the full range of services available in hospital – whether acute or community hospital – are not always needed, and 'intermediate' services can be used instead.

36. Intermediate services can play a key role, but their purpose has to be clear. The term 'intermediate' is often used in a confusing way and is applied at different times to different services, settings or roles. It is used in this report for services that provide rehabilitation between hospital and home. Such services provide rehabilitation to people who are medically stable, but who are not yet ready to return home after their discharge from hospital. They can also be used as 'step-up' facilities for people living at home who need a period of intensive rehabilitation, but who do not need the full range of inpatient services with specialist medical and nursing support on site. The key distinction between inpatient rehabilitation services and intermediate rehabilitation services is therefore the presence in the former of specialist clinical support on site. If this is not made clear, there is a danger that given the general confusion around the term 'intermediate care', older people will not receive the care that they need. Those who are not medically stable may be discharged inappropriately to a setting without clinical support, or they may be transferred to 'intermediate' inpatient beds off the main hospital site – such as those in small community hospitals – without either intensive rehabilitation or specialist clinical care.

Some areas appear to rely entirely on hospitals to provide rehabilitation.

37. The development of intermediate services is somewhat controversial. Some people fear that with the confusion surrounding the concept, older people will be excluded from the appropriate specialist medical and other resources they need, in order to clear hospital beds. In practice, a mixed economy is needed that includes sufficient inpatient rehabilitation services for older people, complete with comprehensive multidisciplinary assessment, specialist medical and nursing input and 'intensive' therapy. However, evidence is growing that some older people can also benefit from services whose primary function is to build their confidence to cope once more with day-to-day activities. If such services are to flourish and be as effective as possible, they need to be planned with the full involvement of those providing specialist services. They need to be closely linked to inpatient services to ensure that people are referred appropriately, and have quick access to specialist medical and other support when needed. In short, they should act as an extension to specialist clinical care and rehabilitation, and not as a substitute for it.

38. One initiative attracting growing attention is the development of social services residential rehabilitation schemes. One-half of the 16 sites visited had established a social rehabilitation scheme [**EXHIBIT 12**]. Two have been operating in Devon for several years [**CASE STUDY 1A**]. Using a short-term stay in a residential setting, the aim is to help frail older people to regain confidence and some of the personal skills lost through acute illness or injury and to avoid unnecessary admissions to long-stay residential or nursing home care.

39. Local evaluations of both schemes reported some very positive results. People initially considered to be on the threshold of admission to long-stay residential or nursing home care were returning home in high numbers with relatively low levels of support. These findings were endorsed by an audit of both schemes by the SSI and the Audit Commission [**CASE STUDY 1B, overleaf**].

EXHIBIT 12

Study site provision

One-half of the sites visited had established a social rehabilitation scheme.

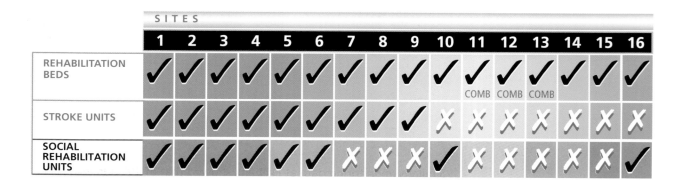

	SITES															
	1	**2**	**3**	**4**	**5**	**6**	**7**	**8**	**9**	**10**	**11**	**12**	**13**	**14**	**15**	**16**
REHABILITATION BEDS	✓	✓	✓	✓	✓	✓	✓	✓	✓	✓	✓ COMB	✓ COMB	✓ COMB	✓	✓	✓
STROKE UNITS	✓	✓	✓	✓	✓	✓	✓	✓	✓	✗	✗	✗	✗	✗	✗	✗
SOCIAL REHABILITATION UNITS	✓	✓	✓	✓	✓	✓	✗	✗	✗	✓	✗	✗	✗	✗	✗	✓

Note: COMB refers only to sites with combined acute and rehabilitation wards.
Source: Audit Commission study site data

CASE STUDY 1A

Social services rehabilitation schemes – Exebank, Exmouth (Devon SSD) and Outlands, Plymouth (Plymouth SSD)

Outlands in Plymouth, Devon began operating in 1992 and Exebank in Exmouth in 1995. Both are short-term residential units that were previously local authority residential homes. Outlands focuses mainly on older people discharged from hospital, while Exebank also takes admissions from people living at home, where the GP confirms that hospital care is not required. Funding comes through social services and health. For example, the health service funds the occupational therapists (OTs) , physiotherapists, rehabilitation assistants and a designated community nurse at Exebank. Additional services are available to Exebank through the local re-ablement team – speech therapist, continence advisor and clinical psychologist. There are 19 beds at Exebank and 23 at Outlands. The average length of stay is just over 29 days at Exebank and 42 days at Outlands.

During the pilot stage of the Outlands project, 42 people were discharged home during a six-month period in 1992/93. While in hospital, all had been assessed as definitely needing admission to residential care. At the time of the pilot, dependency was measured against a core assessment format (assessing mobility, personal care, etc) and showed an average improvement of 28 per cent when people were discharged home. A follow-up exercise was carried out from March to June 1997. Of the 42 people, 22 had died (often after quite lengthy periods at home) but only 4 had been admitted to residential or nursing home care during the 5 year period (Ref. 22). Finally, levels of ongoing domiciliary care at home were found to be low. In addition a separate telephone survey of 90 users in July 1995 indicated that 45 per cent did not need continuing social care support. The SSI estimated that an average ongoing home-care package cost about £50 per week.

Similarly, monitoring data at Exebank showed that of 105 admissions in 1996, 86 per cent were admitted from hospital. At the point of referral, 24 per cent were assessed as having the potential to return home, but once the rehabilitation programme was completed, over 71 per cent actually went home (Ref. 23).

CASE STUDY 1B

Audit Commission/SSI audit of two social services rehabilitation schemes – Exebank, Exmouth (Devon SSD) and Outlands, Plymouth (Plymouth SSD)

The audit was designed to provide information on three questions:

- Are the schemes taking people who would otherwise have been admitted to residential or nursing homes?

- Do such people return home?

- For those who do return home, is the result long term?

Method

Given that Outlands and Exebank operate to the same overall aims, the two settings were considered together. A 20 per cent systematic sample of clients was drawn from a full chronological list of discharges from both units for the period 22 April 1996 to 21 April 1998. The sample was stratified so that 20 per cent of the discharges were drawn from each unit, providing 70 discharges from Outlands and 49 from Exebank, or 119 overall.

Casefiles of the sample of clients were reviewed and information drawn from them to ascertain:

- whether there was sufficient evidence that the client had been on the threshold of admission to residential or nursing home care (final judgement lay with the SSI inspector); and

- the care package provided at the time of discharge.

Findings

It was judged that 72 out of the 119 users (60.5 per cent) had been on the threshold of entering residential or nursing home care when they entered these schemes.

Of these 72 cases, 1 had died and 1 had withdrawn from the scheme, while 16 were admitted to a residential/ nursing home or hospital. A statistical analysis showed that the effect of the scheme is real at the point of discharge.

The effect of the scheme was found to be lasting and people discharged were still significantly independent on follow-up at 1 March 1998.

Ideally, the scheme should have been assessed prospectively using a randomised control trial or a matched-pair sampling methodology. Users would either have been allocated to the scheme (test group), or to a comparison scheme (control group). The outcomes for each (randomised or matched pair) group of users could then have been compared. Such an approach was not possible in the time, but the audit did provide useful information about the operation of the schemes.

40. While the overall evidence showed that the schemes were successful, some important issues were raised. Firstly, a high number of people (nearly 40 per cent) going through the schemes were not considered to be on the threshold of admission to long-term care when initially admitted. While these people may well have benefited from the services, the schemes were specifically set up for people on the threshold of long-term care. Their presence within the schemes in such high numbers shows how easy it is for services to shift from their original aims and purpose. If planned and understood, such a shift is fine. If not, people who are on the threshold of admission to long-stay care may be denied access. Such services need to be continually monitored and evaluated to ensure that people receiving care meet the eligibility criteria, and that the aims and objectives of the schemes are being achieved.

41. Secondly, the Devon schemes and their success need to be understood in the context of the local arrangements. The schemes are well integrated into the range of other rehabilitation services available in the locality, and a number of systems and processes support their success. In both areas of Devon there are a range of well-developed and integrated rehabilitation services across health and social care. Particularly important are:

- a clear set of arrangements for gatekeeping and accessing the service, which is linked with, and related to, all other rehabilitation services in the area and in both cases, the local consultant geriatricians are closely involved with the schemes;

- a range of rehabilitation services available to support people after discharge from the social rehabilitation scheme, provided by the local re-ablement team; and

- a record of evaluation of the schemes (monitoring is particularly well developed at Exebank), so that the services are continually reviewed and refocused as appropriate.

42. Thirdly, it is important that such schemes are properly planned. A recent seminar (Ref. 24) involving staff from intermediate rehabilitation schemes that had been running for some time identified some of the factors that are important when establishing and running such schemes:

- create a separate therapeutic physical environment;

- involve appropriate staff (OTs, physiotherapists and care staff) to create a therapeutic approach through a dedicated team;

- plan a sustainable catchment area (important when linking to GPs and primary care);

- have an appropriate number of beds planned in the context of other rehabilitation services for older people in the area;

- support staff through appropriate training and team building;

- have clear eligibility criteria and gatekeeping protocols (particularly checking that information is available on prognosis, medical stability and motivation);

- promote the service so that staff in all agencies understand its role and focus;

- involve users and carers in the rehabilitation programme by sharing and agreeing goals; and

- have clear information about charges for users.

43. Schemes established by other authorities are now also reporting encouraging findings from early evaluations. For example, a recently established scheme in Rotherham has been evaluated by the University of York Health Economics Consortium [CASE STUDY 2, overleaf]. The scheme achieves similar rates of return home to the Devon schemes and the evaluation concludes that 'the scheme is cost effective for the NHS and Social Services'.

CASE STUDY 2

Rotherham – residential rehabilitation scheme

Rotherham has used short-stay residential home places with intensive therapy input, both as a step between acute hospital and home, and to prevent admission to hospital. The scheme is modelled on the 'Outlands' project in Devon. It was established in surplus accommodation in Broom Hayes, part of Rothwell Grange, a social services residential home. Initially, the scheme had six places, but was subsequently extended to nine. The facility is managed by social services but additional therapy staff have been provided by the NHS. Based on a multidisciplinary assessment of individual need, the aim of the unit is 'to provide therapy, care and support to enable older people to achieve their maximum level of independence'. Residents need to be medically stable. Intensive residential rehabilitation is provided for a maximum of six weeks. On discharge, the progress of residents who return to their own homes is monitored over a six-month period.

The cost of the scheme is shared between health and social services. The NHS meets the costs of physio and occupational therapy and the overall management of the scheme. Social services meet the cost of a hospital-based social worker, scheme-based social workers and day-to-day unit running costs, including care staff.

The scheme has been evaluated by the University of York Health Economics Consortium (Ref. 25). A total of 50 patients were admitted to Broom Hayes in the fist 9 months of operation, with 34 rejections after assessment. Of those admitted, 82 per cent were 75 or above (50 per cent were 85 or over). Only one person was under 65. Of those admitted, 80 per cent lived alone. Almost two-thirds of assessments were undertaken on a hospital ward and one-third in people's own homes. Almost all assessments were undertaken by two or more professionals (82 out of 84). A physiotherapist was involved in 93 per cent of assessments, an OT in 82 per cent and a social worker in 60 per cent.

The average length of stay was 22 days and only 2 patients stayed beyond 6 weeks. Patients were assessed against a dependency scoring system on admission and at discharge. The profiles of the dependency scores indicated that the majority of improvement was achieved within the first four weeks with some requiring less time to restore their independence. This indicates 'the importance of having individual plans for each resident rather than a standard period of residence for everyone' (Ref. 25).

In total, 39 people out of 50 (78 per cent) were discharged home, with only 3 needing admission to long-term care, while 8 had to be admitted or re-admitted to hospital. Of those discharged home, 76 per cent received at least one community service, 46 per cent received two or more services and 18 per cent at least three services.

Six months after discharge, 71 per cent of those discharged home were still at home.

The evaluation concluded that the scheme is cost effective for the NHS and Social Services. At 70 per cent occupancy 'the average cost of the NHS therapeutic input is £529 per patient, which is equivalent to about 4 inpatient days at £125 a day'. Assuming that Social Services would need to meet two-thirds of the weekly cost of 24-hour residential care and that three-quarters continue to return home, the break even point occurs for Social Services after recipients have been in the community for between 13 and 18.5 weeks (based on 70 per cent and 50 per cent occupancy levels respectively). Therefore, the scheme has the potential to generate significant cost savings for Social Services.

44. Another recently established scheme in North Yorkshire also reports a high rate of discharge home for frail older people who, on admission, were assessed as needing long-term care. Again, the initial calculations of the financial, as well as human benefits, are encouraging [**CASE STUDY 3**].

CASE STUDY 3

North Yorkshire pilot social rehabilitation scheme – Scarborough

All 63 admissions to the unit during the first few months of 1999 were assessed as 'requiring some form of residential care'. The average length of stay on the unit was 22 days. Of the 63:

- 7 had to be re-admitted to hospital;
- 6 were discharged to residential or nursing home care; and
- 50 were discharged home.

Of the 50 who were discharged home:

- 30 did not need any services in November 1999;
- 13 received 'low' packages of care (typical net cost £50 a week); and
- 7 received more expensive packages of care (£75 to £266 net cost a week).

This means that initial net savings (after the costs of the rehabilitation and ongoing community services) of an estimated £41,000 have been achieved, compared with the equivalent cost of independent residential care costs. The scheme is to be closely monitored to see if the benefits can be sustained over the longer term.

Social rehabilitation schemes provide continuing access to therapy in a caring environment.

45. These social rehabilitation schemes provide similar levels of qualified therapy to residents to those provided within health settings **[EXHIBIT 13]**. They also use therapy assistants to increase therapeutic activity. For people who are medically stable and not in need of specialist nursing care, such schemes can be an important way to obtain continuing access to therapy in a caring environment.

46. This is all achieved at relatively low cost. The costs of social rehabilitation units are about one-half of those of community hospitals according to research commissioned for the study, looking at the rehabilitation pathways and costs of patients with a fractured neck of femur **[BOX B]**. The research has shown that length of stay dominates the total costs. Patients who are transferred to either a community hospital or social rehabilitation scheme have a longer overall length of stay and thus total costs are higher, than those who remain in acute care, despite higher daily costs. This reiterates the importance of ensuring that the use of intermediate settings is appropriately targeted at those who would otherwise be unable to return home.

EXHIBIT 13

Qualified therapy time: available occupational therapy and physiotherapy minutes per bed per day in social rehabilitation schemes.

Social rehabilitation schemes provide similar levels of therapy to residents within health settings.

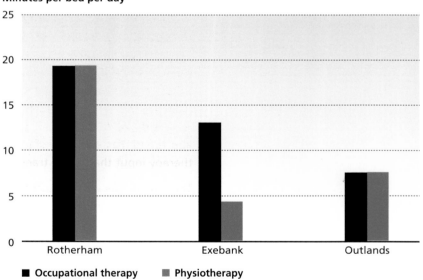

Minutes per bed per day

■ **Occupational therapy** ■ **Physiotherapy**

Source: Data from the Rotherham, Plymouth and Exmouth schemes

47. Being 'social' rehabilitation schemes, run by local authorities, users were charged for their short-term residential stay. However, these data show that users were accessing NHS-funded and provided therapy in a caring and homely environment. In the light of this, the issue of charging needs to be reviewed, if such schemes are to develop and play as effective a role as they could.

BOX B

Rehabilitation Pathways for Older People. Research into pathways and costs. Nuffield Institute for Health, University of Leeds, with the University of York (Ref. 26)

The Audit Commission commissioned research from the University of York with the Nuffield Institute for Health at the University of Leeds to look at rehabilitation pathways for older people, using fractured neck of femur as a tracer condition. The research investigated the experiences of people and the costs of care at four sites. The research found that the rehabilitation inputs varied between sites and individuals, even between people with apparently similar levels of need.

The use of community hospitals was not always justified in relation to the need for specialist medical cover through a period of recovery. Those in hospital on some sites were at similar levels of need to those in other sites who were discharged into other models of care – for example, social rehabilitation units. This is despite costs of £59 a day net (£66.50 gross) for an actual scheme compared to community hospital costs of £123 a day. For example, in one area (of three reviewed) people were placed in each type of care depending on where they lived rather than by need. The research also found that those transferred to a community hospital received lower therapy input than those transferred to social rehabilitation units.

The environment within some community hospitals and all the social rehabilitation units was felt to be more homely by users, and the attitude of staff more tolerant of higher levels of need than in acute wards. People were very complimentary about their treatment in social care settings.

Source: Nuffield Institute for Health, University of Leeds, with the University of York (Ref. 26).

Day and community-based services

48. Day hospitals are available in many areas and are seen as a resource for assessment and rehabilitation. Community-based assessment and rehabilitation services need to be available to:

- help avoid admission to hospital in situations where appropriate assessment and care can be provided in the community; and

- provide assessment, rehabilitation and review in people's own homes.

49. Once again, it is important that people are clear about the focus and role of services. Nearly all of the sites visited had a day hospital, but only just over one-third had a multidisciplinary team providing assessment and rehabilitation in the community [**EXHIBIT 14**].

50. Audit Commission locality data also indicate that a day hospital is available in 80 per cent of localities and access to multidisciplinary teams in 50 per cent. However, again, this is only part of the story. The absence of intermediate and community-based services in many areas in the past has meant that day services, particularly day hospitals, have been the only resource for accessing multidisciplinary assessment, rehabilitation and review outside an inpatient setting. However, day hospitals are used in many different ways, and reviews have indicated that some are not used well because of poor co-ordination, inadequate transport arrangements and poor overall use of time. They are relatively expensive and people spend a lot of time travelling to them.

EXHIBIT 14

Study site provision

Nearly all of the sites visited had a day hospital, but only just over one-third had a multidisciplinary team providing assessment and rehabilitation in the community.

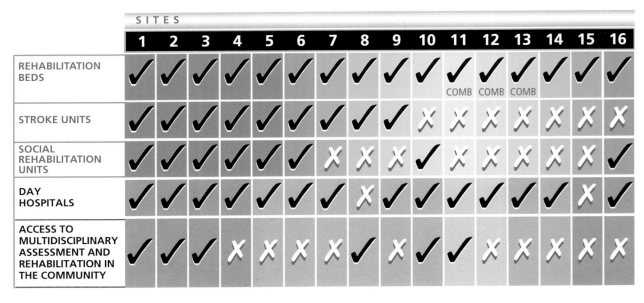

Note: COMB refers only to sites with combined acute and rehabilitation wards.

Source: Audit Commission study site data

51. Access to day hospitals and home-based teams by older people varies by locality. The number of new users aged 75 or over accessing day hospitals varies by more than a factor of ten and by even more for home-based multidisciplinary rehabilitation [**EXHIBIT 15**]. The result is different patterns of use – some focus on reviews while others focus more on active rehabilitation. Again, this is fine as long as people are clear about their role and purpose within the wider range of rehabilitation services.

EXHIBIT 15

Number of new users aged 75 or over per 10,000 population aged 75 or over

The number of new users aged 75 or over varies more than tenfold for day hospitals...

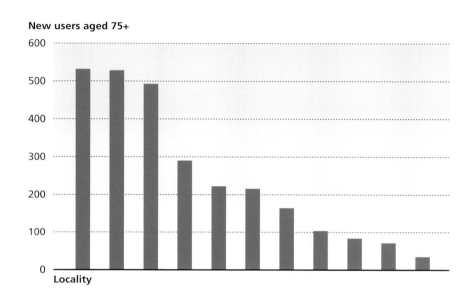

New users aged 75+

Locality

... and by significantly more for home-based multidisciplinary rehabilitation.

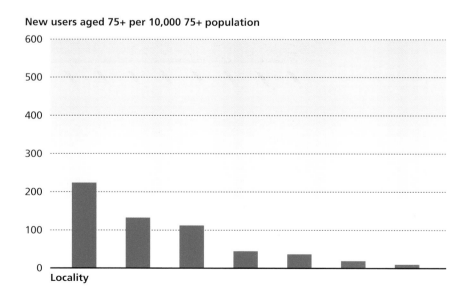

New users aged 75+ per 10,000 75+ population

Locality

Source: Audit Commission locality data collection

The majority... of community rehabilitation teams... have some physiotherapy and OT input, but there are significant gaps from other professions.

52. Community rehabilitation, starting from a low base, has been growing rapidly. A recent postal survey of 98 community rehabilitation teams by Professor Pam Enderby of Sheffield University (Ref. 27), has found that many do not have representatives from key professions. The majority have some physiotherapy and OT input, but there are significant gaps from other professions [**EXHIBIT 16**]. Physiotherapy was available to 94 per cent of teams and occupational therapy to 92 per cent, but nursing input was available to only 43 per cent, speech and language therapy to only 39 per cent and medical input to only 27 per cent. Indeed, in many cases, the teams were no more than community therapy teams rather than full multidisciplinary rehabilitation teams. This is not to say that they do not provide a useful service, but they further reflect the confusion surrounding the nature of rehabilitation services, especially given that the survey found that 58 per cent of teams were developed to facilitate early discharge, 29 per cent were to help close hospital facilities, and only 13 per cent were an 'additional service development'. Commenting on this, Professor Enderby noted that nursing and medical involvement were key to the service being replaced, but in nearly all cases they were not included in the community team. In addition, more than 50 per cent of teams had time-limited funding and their future was not secure.

EXHIBIT 16

Multidisciplinary involvement in community rehabilitation teams

The majority have some physiotherapy and occupational therapy input, but there are significant gaps from other professions.

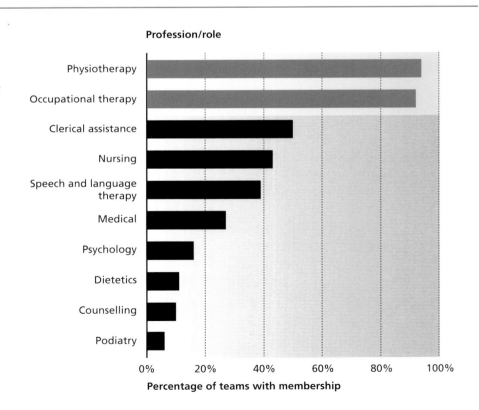

Profession/role

Percentage of teams with membership

Source: Professor Pam Enderby: A survey of community rehabilitation teams (Ref. 27)

53. A clear purpose, and the staffing to meet that purpose, are essential. In Rotherham, a Community Assessment Rehabilitation and Treatment Scheme (CARATS) has been developed. Part of its purpose was to provide a rapid response scheme in the community to prevent avoidable admissions to hospital, reduce lengths of stay in acute hospital care and prevent inappropriate admissions to residential and nursing homes. By being clear about the role and purpose of the scheme, and linking it to other initiatives, independent evaluation has shown that considerable benefits have accrued [CASE STUDY 4].

CASE STUDY 4

Rotherham – Community Assessment Rehabilitation and Treatment Scheme (CARATS)

Between 1990/91 and 1994/95 Rotherham Acute Trust experienced a 32 per cent growth in emergencies and an 85 per cent increase in admissions through A&E. A review of inpatient and other facilities in general medicine and medicine for the elderly (Ref. 28) showed that an additional 14 beds were required. Predicted demographic change suggested that the Trust would need another 29 beds (ie, another ward) by the year 2000 unless alternatives to hospital care were developed locally.

The response was to develop a Community Assessment, Rehabilitation and Treatment Scheme (CARATS) in 1997, using money from the Continuing Care Challenge Fund. CARATS was developed by local NHS and social services organisations to:

- prevent avoidable admissions to hospital;
- reduce lengths of stay in acute hospital care;
- prevent inappropriate admissions to residential/ nursing home care;

- devolve care assessment and management of these patients to the primary care team; and
- help to identify local community care needs.

Initially, the scheme was made up of two major elements:

- a 'fast response service'; and
- residential and day rehabilitation schemes.

The University of York Health Economics Consortium has evaluated both (Ref. 25).

The rapid response team received 644 referrals in its first 15 months of operation, with 406 being accepted. Approximately twice as many accepted referrals were to prevent admission than to facilitate discharge, and increasing numbers of assessments were undertaken in the community. Terminally ill patients accounted for about 40 per cent of accepted referrals. Only 8 per cent of patients had to be admitted to hospital while in receipt of CARATS. Considerable numbers of bed days have been saved (1,684–2,880 depending on assumptions about

length of stay), at a lower cost per bed day.

In addition to the two major elements of CARATS, other schemes have been developed. These have included:

- the provision of therapy (physio- and occupational therapy) to a social services day centre to complement the social rehabilitation scheme; and
- the use of nursing home beds for recovery. These were for patients who no longer required hospital-based medical care but who needed a maximum two-week period of nurse-supported care and recovery before returning home. They were also used to prevent hospital admission for people whose carer had fallen ill.

In addition, other developments are being planned as there is still considerable potential to improve the schemes further and to extend the range of care provided in patients' homes.

...often missing from community-based approaches is full and speedy access to medical assessment and care...

54. In Sheffield, a well established set of community rehabilitation teams (CRTs) have been developed [CASE STUDY 5]. While based in the community, they have good links with acute care and local inpatient rehabilitation services and have access to intensive home-care nursing.

55. The most critical element often missing from community-based approaches is full and speedy access to medical assessment and care, linked to all the other multidisciplinary inputs. A full multidisciplinary approach to community-based rehabilitation has been taken in North Devon with the development of community re-ablement teams [CASE STUDY 6A].

CASE STUDY 5

Sheffield community rehabilitation teams (CRTs)

Two community rehabilitation teams (CRTs) were established in 1995 in Sheffield as a partnership between the community health trust and the two acute trusts to provide therapy within patients' homes. They were established as part of a reconfiguration of services and as a direct alternative to multidisciplinary therapy in hospital. A third and a fourth team were established in January 1999. The CRTs now cover all patients who have a GP in Sheffield.

There are two teams covering the north of the city and two covering the south. Core membership comprises two physiotherapists, two OTs, generic therapy assistants, a speech and language therapist, and administrative/ clerical staff. There is a dedicated social worker and psychologist covering all four teams. There are two team leaders; a physiotherapist covering the two northern teams and an OT covering the two southern teams. Access to 48 hours of intensive home-care nursing is available. The CRT has its own equipment store, and team members can visit patients on the day of discharge.

Team working is aided by weekly meetings to set and review joint therapy and patient goals. Team members also meet up at the beginning and end of each working day. Patient-held records are also maintained. CRT members treat patients for up to three months and will visit and review the patient three months after discharge. Each team can treat approximately 22–25 patients at any one time depending on case mix.

56. Evidence suggests that the re-ablement model is proving successful in meeting its objectives. It is making a major contribution not only to the delivery of well-managed, co-ordinated assessment and rehabilitation, but to the management of demand across the health and social care economy. Two similar general practices in the area have been compared – one with access to re-ablement and the other without access [CASE STUDY 6B, overleaf]. The practice with access has seen a fall in emergency admissions for people over 75, in length of hospital stay and the percentage of re-admissions while the other has seen a rise in these measures [EXHIBIT 17, overleaf]. Overall, the Northern Devon Healthcare Trust reported a 12 per cent drop in emergency admissions at a time when most others are experiencing a rise.

CASE STUDY 6A

North Devon Re-ablement Teams

The reablement service provides multidisciplinary rehabilitation in the community to all people over 16. Partnership Grant monies have been used to fund social services staff. Social re-ablement beds are also available.

Currently, there are four teams – based in Ilfracombe, Barnstaple, Bideford and Holsworthy. A fifth team is planned for South Molton.

The aims of the re-ablement service are to:

- reduce the number of avoidable emergency and unplanned admissions and re-admissions to hospital;

- ensure people are discharged from hospital in a timely and effective manner;

- reduce the number of long-term placements in residential and nursing care by 20 per cent per annum; and

- ensure that the services provided to maintain people at home are well targeted and effective.

Referrals can be made by anyone. The teams have physiotherapy, occupational therapy, speech and language therapy, nurses, medical sessions, support workers/community care workers, a social worker, a co-ordinator and administration/clerical support. In addition, the team provides access to a psychologist, dieticians, a chiropodist, primary care services and a volunteers' co-ordinator.

Admission to the re-ablement beds for a planned maximum of six to eight weeks allows proper assessment of needs and appropriate planning. These beds may be needed where:

- a carer becomes incapacitated and there is no immediately obvious replacement and the patient is at risk or at potential risk;

- any incident at home renders it unsafe for the person to stay at home; and

- an acute problem occurs but it is not appropriate to admit to hospital. However, there may be a short-term increase in care needs due to loss of confidence or increased physical need in the short term.

Community re-ablement contributes to the delivery of well-managed, co-ordinated assessment and rehabilitation...and ...to the management of demand across the health and social care economy.

CASE STUDY 6B

North Devon Re-ablement Team – key success data

Details on the North Devon Re-ablement Teams have been given in Case Studies 6A (location,staffing and aims), 9 (key worker system) and 10 (team working). There is encouraging evidence that the teams are delivering outcomes in line with the aims and objectives. In doing so, the re-ablement service is making a major contribution not only to the delivery of well-managed, co-ordinated assessment and rehabilitation, but to the management of demand across the health and social care economy.

To evaluate the impact of re-ablement two general practices of equal size and demographic composition were compared.

	Practice A	Practice B
Number of GPs	6	6
Number of community hospital beds	14	18
Number of nursing beds	165	177
Number of residential beds	289	236
Total	**454**	**413**
Total number of patients	**8865**	**7723**
Total number of patients aged over 75	840	758
Total number (percentage) of patients aged over 75	9.5%	9.8%

Practice A had access to re-ablement from 1994, whereas Practice B did not have access until 1999. Data for those aged over 75 were collated and compared for 1992 (when neither had access to re-ablement) and for 1998 (when Practice A had had access to re-ablement for over three years). This covered emergency stays in hospital, the average length of stay for patients admitted, the re-admission rate and occupied bed days. The comparison shows an improving pattern for practice A with access to reablement and deterioration for practice B without access [EXHIBIT 17]. Between 1992 and 1998, Practice A with re-ablement saw a reduction for the over 75s in emergency admissions, in length of hospital stay and the percentage of re-admissions. Conversely, Practice B saw an increase for the over 75s in emergency admissions, in length of hospital stay and the percentage of re-admissions.

EXHIBIT 17

Comparison of two similar general practices

The practice with access to re-ablement has seen a fall in emergency admissions, re-admissions and lengths of stay while the other has seen a rise.

Percentage or number

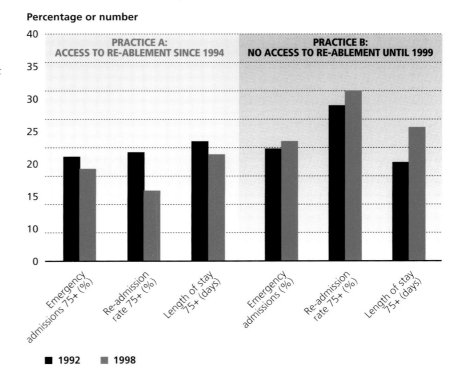

■ 1992　■ 1998

Source: Data from North and East Devon Health Authority and Northern Devon Healthcare Trust

57. Day care can also be used to provide rehabilitation. At the Oaks Resource Centre in Bradford, therapy is used to help older people keep their independence and live in their own homes in the community for as long as possible [**CASE STUDY 7**, overleaf].

CASE STUDY 7

Bradford – The Oaks Resource Centre (Keighley)

The Oaks is a day centre run by Bradford Social Services offering social day care, therapy and support to older people in Keighley and surrounding areas of West Yorkshire. The centre aims to help people to keep their independence and live in their own homes in the community for as long as possible.

A range of services is jointly provided by Bradford Social Services and Airedale NHS Trust, including 15 places per day for older people who need physiotherapy and occupational therapy as part of their rehabilitation following injury or illness. The building has a new fully equipped occupational therapy and physiotherapy department. A range of other services is also available including bathing, chiropody and counselling. Those attending have care programmes drawn up in full discussion with both themselves and their carers. The programmes are reviewed regularly. Each person has a 'key worker' who is responsible for co-ordinating their care. Once the care programme has been completed, a review is held to decide whether further rehabilitation or day care is needed.

Currently, the centre is only open on weekdays but funding is being sought to extend the opening hours to weekends.

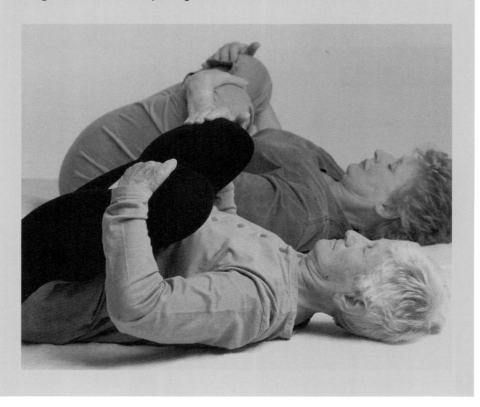

Linking services

58. So far, individual services have been described. However, such services should not exist in isolation, but be part of a whole system. In most areas, the services reflect historical rather than planned development, producing very different patterns overall, with significant gaps in the services available in some areas **[EXHIBIT 14, p30]**. A first important link is that between initial 'acute' care and inpatient rehabilitation. Although all sites had inpatient rehabilitation beds, the type and location of those beds varied **[EXHIBIT 18]**. Eight had rehabilitation beds on the acute site, with three having combined acute and rehabilitation beds. Five had rehabilitation beds provided on a different site, and two had provision both 'on' and 'off' site. This has particular significance to the management of patient pathways as discussed in Chapter 3.

59. The diversity in the range of services available and the overall arrangements at different sites can be illustrated by showing the very different service configurations in four areas.

EXHIBIT 18

Type and location of rehabilitation beds

The type and location of rehabilitation beds varied.

SITES WITH REHABILITATION BEDS FOR OLDER PEOPLE

of these...

3 COMBINED ACUTE/ REHABILITATION BEDS

5 SEPARATE BEDS BASED ON 'ACUTE' SITES

5 SEPARATE REHABILITATION BEDS BASED 'OFF SITE'

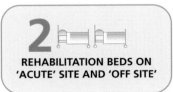

2 REHABILITATION BEDS ON 'ACUTE' SITE AND 'OFF SITE'

Source: Audit Commission study site data

60. In Area A, services are quite limited and there are significant gaps [**EXHIBIT 19**]. After acute care, inpatient rehabilitation beds are available on the same site in two wards of 20 beds with some access to a high-dependency unit off site. There is no stroke rehabilitation unit. A limited amount of rehabilitation is available in two intermediate settings, provided by a nursing home and social services. There is a day hospital available for follow up and therapy. There are no community-based therapy services available for people in their own homes.

EXHIBIT 19

Rehabilitation services for older people in Area A

Services are quite limited and there are significant gaps.

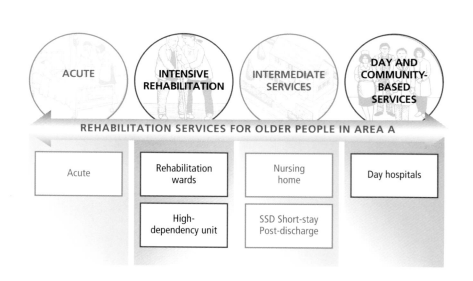

Source: Audit Commission study site data

61. In Area B, services are more extensive than in Area A, but there are some gaps, particularly in intermediate and community services **[EXHIBIT 20]**. There is a high number of options immediately after acute care with inpatient rehabilitation beds on other sites. Although immediate acute stroke care is spread across all general medical wards, there is a stroke rehabilitation unit. There are adult general rehabilitation and elderly care rehabilitation beds, and a specific orthogeriatric facility. All of these are hospital based with specialist medical and nursing input available. There are no intermediate facilities for those who require therapeutic input but not specialist medical or nursing input on site. There is no social rehabilitation unit. There is a day hospital and community-based physiotherapy and occupational therapy, but no access for older people to the full range of services required for community-based multidisciplinary assessment and rehabilitation.

EXHIBIT 20

Rehabilitation services for older people in Area B

Services are more extensive than in Area A but with some gaps particularly in intermediate and community services.

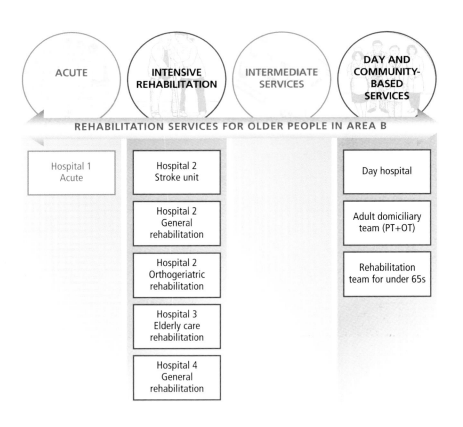

Source: Audit Commission study site data

62. In Area C, services are quite developed, with an increasing range of services available in the community [**EXHIBIT 21**]. Acute and intensive rehabilitation services are provided from the same site with a well-differentiated set of 'intensive' rehabilitation services, provided under specialist medical and nursing cover. These include separate wards for stroke rehabilitation, orthogeriatric rehabilitation, and the rehabilitation of frail older people in general rehabilitation wards with other adults. There is also a ward, under the supervision of a geriatrician, that prepares older people who are going to need to enter long-term care, following a full multidisciplinary assessment. There is a social rehabilitation unit available in one part of the city, but no other significant 'intermediate facilities'. There is a day hospital and a well-developed set of multidisciplinary community rehabilitation teams, with social services involvement, working in older people's own homes.

EXHIBIT 21

Rehabilitation services for older people in Area C

Services are quite developed and there is an increasing range of services available in the community.

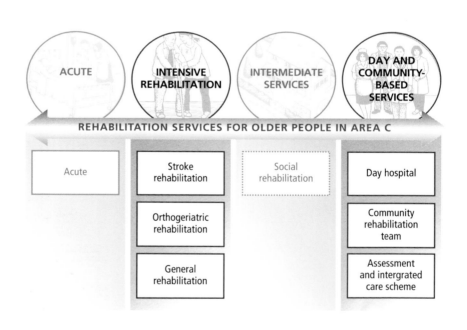

Source: Audit Commission study site data

63. In Area D, services are well developed and integrated, with a significant involvement by both social and health services [EXHIBIT 22]. After acute care there is a stroke rehabilitation unit off site and elderly care rehabilitation wards all providing rehabilitation services under specialist medical and nursing care. There is also a well-developed range of 'intermediate' services for those who are medically stable but who require more time, care and therapy to recover fully. These include a social rehabilitation unit and other health units all with a clear purpose. Finally, day and community rehabilitation services are well developed, with a day hospital, a rapid response team and a community re-ablement team. The re-ablement team is critical. As well as providing multidisciplinary care in people's own homes, it is available to work with patients in the intermediate settings, providing reliable and quick access to specialist medical and other input where necessary.

Conclusion

64. All areas have some rehabilitation services, but most have gaps. Services have been developed in isolation, and need to be reviewed together. They also need to have clear links between them, and this is the subject of the next chapter.

EXHIBIT 22

Rehabilitation services for older people in Area D

Services are well developed and integrated with a significant involvement by social services and health.

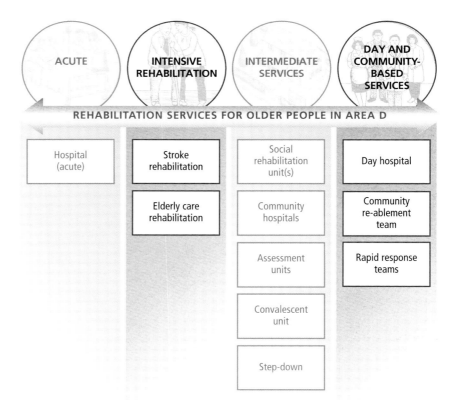

REHABILITATION SERVICES FOR OLDER PEOPLE IN AREA D

ACUTE	INTENSIVE REHABILITATION	INTERMEDIATE SERVICES	DAY AND COMMUNITY-BASED SERVICES
Hospital (acute)	Stroke rehabilitation	Social rehabilitation unit(s)	Day hospital
	Elderly care rehabilitation	Community hospitals	Community re-ablement team
		Assessment units	Rapid response teams
		Convalescent unit	
		Step-down	

Source: Audit Commission study site data

RECOMMENDATIONS

2 The Provision of Rehabilitation Services

1 Authorities and trusts need to be clear about the role and nature of inpatient rehabilitation beds provided for older people.

2 Trusts that do not have stroke units should be setting them up in accordance with the research evidence.

3 Authorities need to consider establishing intermediate rehabilitation services, integrating them into the range of other rehabilitation services.

4 Community-based assessment and rehabilitation services are needed to support people in the community, but teams need to be clear about their purpose and be staffed accordingly.

5 Individual services should not exist in isolation, but be part of a coherent whole.

6 Agencies in each area need to review the overall pattern of services and work out whether some reconfiguration is desirable.

3

Managing the Rehabilitation Programme

People need to follow a clear care pathway while receiving rehabilitation. These arrangements require good co-ordination and multidisciplinary working.

65. Effective organisation and co-ordination of the rehabilitation programme is crucial. Many older people who require help have a number of problems – possibly more than one medical condition requiring lots of different drugs (multiple pathology and polypharmacy). Many have a physical disability and a high number have dementia. A proportion have difficulties with their social and environmental support.

66. If older people's level of functioning is to be restored to the maximum extent possible, a whole range of needs will have to be addressed. For some people, the process will be complex and time consuming, and will involve a range of different services provided by different professionals and organisations. This chapter examines the arrangements needed to make this happen, looking first at the care pathways that need to be in place, and then at how staff need to work together to use these pathways to best effect.

Care pathways

67. People who need intensive rehabilitation need to follow a clear pathway that involves screening, assessment, care planning and good continuity when transfers occur between services.

Screening

68. The first stage of the process is to identify the people who need an intensive programme of rehabilitation. An effective screening process is required to identify them either on the wards or at home. Without good screening systems, wrong decisions become more likely. On busy acute wards, older people's needs can be missed in the constant pressure to discharge or transfer patients as quickly as possible. They may be considered 'safe' to be discharged home, or to require a residential or nursing home placement before a proper assessment of their rehabilitation potential has been made. Alternatively, pressure to free up beds may lead to patients being transferred to an available bed on a rehabilitation ward inappropriately, while they are still too ill to be able to participate in active rehabilitation.

69. The screening of older people's needs for rehabilitation is particularly important where they are admitted to general wards throughout the hospital and integrated with younger people. Greater integration can have positive benefits, but it can also mean that people who would benefit from 'concentrated' care by a specialist team – people who have had a stroke, for example – are not easy to reach. Of the hospitals studied, one-third concentrated acute care for stroke patients in a defined set of beds or wards. The other two-thirds admitted stroke patients to a wide range of locations throughout the hospital. Direct comparison of the distribution of stroke patients three days after admission in two different hospitals illustrates this point. Where stroke patients tended to be concentrated in Hospital A, they were admitted across 16 different wards in Hospital B – making concentrated stroke care difficult and the need for effective screening critical [EXHIBIT 23].

Comprehensive assessment… reduces the risk of older people being re-admitted to hospitals or placed in care homes.

70. A screening form developed in Sheffield helps staff to identify people who need more thorough multidisciplinary assessment **[CASE STUDY 8, overleaf]**. In Bradford, the stroke unit, which operates on a different site from that used for acute medical admissions, employs 'liaison nurses' who 'case find' and carry out pretransfer assessments following an agreed protocol for admission to the stroke unit **[CASE STUDY 11, p60]**.

Assessment

71. Once people who could benefit from intensive rehabilitation have been identified, they then need a multidisciplinary assessment. There is strong evidence that a comprehensive assessment, followed by the development and implementation of individual care plans, reduces the risk of older people being re-admitted to hospitals or placed in care homes. It also improves people's survival rates and their physical and cognitive functioning (Ref. 29). Comprehensive geriatric assessments reduce death rates by 35 per cent and subsequent admissions to hospital by 12 per cent (Ref. 30). Effects of this magnitude are greater than those seen for many accepted drug treatments (Ref. 17). Assessment is crucial to the overall success of the rehabilitation process.

EXHIBIT 23

Location of stroke patients aged 75 or over 3 days after their stroke

Hospital B had stroke patients on 16 different wards.

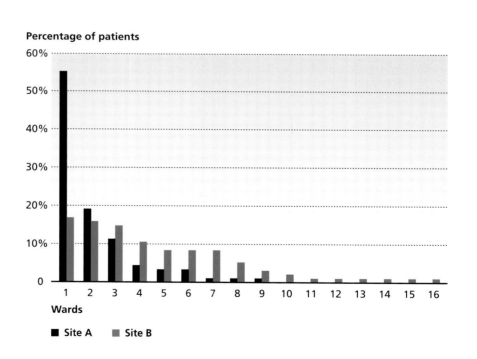

Percentage of patients

Wards

■ Site A ■ Site B

Source: Audit Commission stroke case analysis

CASE STUDY 8

Sheffield standardised screening assessment

The standardised screening assessment has three components:

- A standardised disability assessment completed by staff on the ward.
- A questionnaire completed by the patient.
- A questionnaire completed by a carer, if relevant.

The ward-based assessment has a range of questions about the patient that cover mobility, continence, the ability to self-medicate, transfer, use toilets and bath or shower, and the ability to maintain personal hygiene, dress, feed themselves and speak. They trigger referrals to physiotherapists, occupational therapists, continence nurses, dieticians and speech and language therapists.

The questionnaire also reviews how well people were managing before admission, looking at their ability to maintain the home, cook, shop, handle money, use the telephone, self-medicate, move around indoors and outdoors, transfer, use the toilet and the bath or shower, manage continence, maintain personal hygiene, dress and feed themselves. It also asks about sight, hearing and mental state. It asks for information on who would give assistance if the patient did have any difficulty in these areas.

The carer questionnaire covers similar issues and enables the carer to express any worries or concerns about the patient's ability to cope. The screening assessment helps to identify and document the patient's needs for a wide range of help, to ensure appropriate referral and to plan adequate discharge arrangements.

72. The processes of screening and assessment are far from systematic, however. Evidence continues to grow that exclusion from rehabilitation services is producing more admissions to residential and nursing homes than is necessary. A detailed audit of nursing home placements in England and Wales (Ref. 31) found that only 60 per cent of older people admitted had had an assessment by a consultant geriatrician or psycho-geriatrician recorded on their files prior to admission. Those from hospital were slightly more likely to have had such an assessment than those from home. Over 90 per cent of the records contained no physiotherapy or occupational therapy reports of pre-admission treatments, pre-admission assessments and post-admission management. If 'the lack of documentation reflects a lack of formal therapy assessment, this would indicate a national failure of multidisciplinary assessment prior to the referral and placement of older people in nursing homes'. The audit concluded that between one in six and one in seven residents were 'misplaced'.

The processes of screening and assessment are far from systematic.

73. Where different agencies carry out assessments, problems occur when each agency uses separate assessment tools leading to repetition and increased costs. Two sites visited during the study were in the process of developing community-based shared assessment protocols but they were very much in a minority. A review of documents used for the comprehensive assessment of older people in 50 local authorities across the UK (Ref. 32), found that very few documents were designed to pick up information on the potential for rehabilitation. Only 24 per cent of forms were used jointly by health and social services, leaving the majority of social services staff to seek specialist assessments from other agencies and professionals where necessary. The review reported a 'marked variation not only in the content of assessment (the information sought about needs and how it is recorded) but also in the form (the personnel involved in conducting the assessment)'. Yet, a number of tools already exist that have been validated and that provide a set of questions that trigger the appropriate multidisciplinary input [**BOX C, overleaf**].

BOX C

Some standardised assessment tools

EASY CARE ELDERLY ASSESSMENT SYSTEM – UK VERSION (1999–2002)

This has been developed by Professor Ian Philp at the University of Sheffield. It:
- is a standardised first stage assessment designed for use in primary care settings by community nurses and social care staff;
- is designed to be short, reliable and valid with potential for cross-cultural use;
- is used at initial contact with an older person; when there are changes to their health or social circumstances; as part of screening; to monitor outcomes of care and when assessing for placement;
- can be adapted through the addition of questions according to local need;
- requires appropriate casework to make the necessary referrals and follow-ups; and
- allows for the aggregation of client data for planning and audit purposes.

THE MINIMUM DATA SET (MDS)

Minimum data sets (MDS) have been developed by an international group of researchers and clinicians in elderly care. MDS are available for:
1. Acute hospital care
2. Rehabilitation/post-acute care
3. Home care
4. Residential home/nursing home

Each:
- covers a broad range of assessment domains;
- is designed so that specific responses to items 'trigger' reference to in-depth assessment protocols and prompt a wider assessment;
- allows for repeated assessment at intervals, allowing changes to be monitored over time to show the outcomes of interventions; and
- enables the aggregation of client data for planning and audit purposes.

ROYAL COLLEGE OF NURSING ASSESSMENT TOOL FOR NURSING OLDER PEOPLE

Developed by the Royal College of Nursing, this:
- is designed for use by nursing staff as part of the overall assessment of a resident in a care home but can be used in the community or in hospital settings;
- enables comprehensive assessment of an older person's health status;
- enables the need for input by a registered nurse to be identified through the application of a stability/predictability matrix;
- allows an estimate to be made of the registered nursing hours required, through the use of a scoring formula;
- enables evidence to be identified that supports decision making and practice;
- contributes to the generation of a care plan; and
- can act as a trigger for further, more specific assessment.

Source: King's Fund (Ref. 33)

Care planning

74. Good care planning should then follow assessment. Older people are central to the process, and yet, a large number of patients in the user survey, 42 per cent (n=161), were not even told what a stroke was while in hospital [**EXHIBIT 24**]. Communication between therapists and older people about their care is also sometimes poor. The user survey asked people how therapists asked them about the sort of help they needed (for example, walking, talking, making tea, sitting, dressing etc). Most (61 per cent) reported good or reasonable levels of communication but a considerable minority (27 per cent) reported poor or very poor communication [**EXHIBIT 25, overleaf**].

75. As rehabilitation is often an active, painful process, the lack of information about the nature of a stroke and consultation about overall goals is striking. Goals agreed with the patient are at the heart of the rehabilitation process. To be successful they should be:

- clear and unambiguous;

- meaningful – appropriate to the problems and circumstances of the patient;

- agreed – negotiated with patient, caregivers and rehabilitation team;

- clearly communicated and written down; and

- realistic – challenging but achievable: not everyone can do everything (Ref. 6).

EXHIBIT 24

Users' views about an explanation of stroke

42 per cent of patients were not even told what a stroke was while in hospital.

Q5 While you were in hospital, did anyone explain to you about what stroke was?

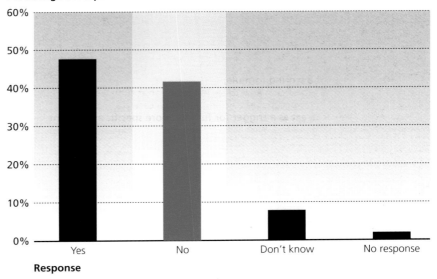

Percentage of respondents

Response

Source: Audit Commission user survey

Communication between therapists and older people about their care is sometimes poor.

76. The central involvement of users in the process is well recognised in therapists' own guidelines on clinical practice. OTs should at all times… acknowledge the need for client choice and the benefits of working in partnership (Ref. 34) and the 'record of recommendations [following an assessment] shall [include] the consumer's goals and/or the goals of his family or carers' (Ref. 35). For physiotherapy, treatment 'plans, goals and predicted outcomes are agreed between the patient and the physiotherapist' (Ref. 36). Although the time pressures on therapists are well recognised, if they do not consult, therapy is not a patient-centred process but a professionally imposed one. In the stroke user survey, a higher proportion of patients treated on stroke units were told about stroke and experienced a significantly better dialogue with therapists.

EXHIBIT 25

Users' views on communication with therapists in hospital

A considerable minority (27 per cent) reported poor or very poor communication.

 When therapists came to see you in hospital, how often did they ask you what things (like walking, talking, making tea, sitting or dressing) you wanted to work hardest on?

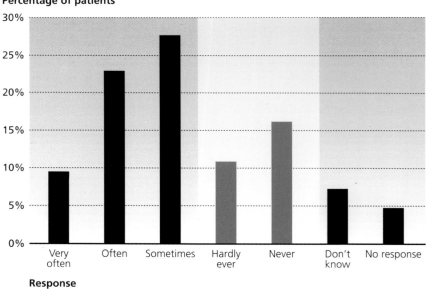

Percentage of patients

Source: Audit Commission user survey

Continuity of care

77. Arrangements for transferring care plans with people when they move between services and organisations need to be clear and in place.

78. While all of the sites visited had rehabilitation beds, the location of these beds differed from site to site. Three sites had combined acute/ rehabilitation beds, five had separate rehabilitation beds on the acute site, five had separate rehabilitation beds off site and two had rehabilitation beds both on the acute site and off site. Critically, for the organisation and management of care, this meant that rehabilitation often involved a transfer – either within a site, or between sites. Sometimes the transfer was between organisations. Despite the number of transfers needed, only one site had a transfer protocol, for one particular service [**EXHIBIT 26**].

EXHIBIT 26

Protocols for the transfer of older people to rehabilitation beds

Despite the need for a high number of transfers, only one site had a transfer protocol, for one particular service.

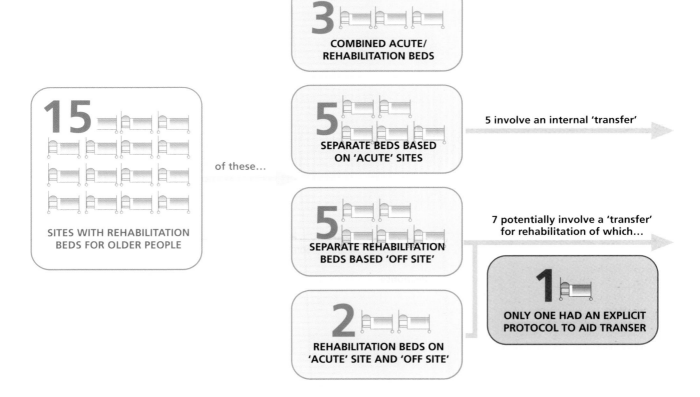

Source: Audit Commission study site data

79. For stroke patients, multidisciplinary teams were predominantly concerned with the management of inpatient rehabilitation. Only three teams provided any ongoing support in day settings or in people's own homes. Yet only three of the other teams had explicit protocols for transferring care plans. This meant that in many cases, continuity of care relied at best on verbal discussions between services or other informal exchanges of information.

80. The user survey found that the shortfalls in the arrangements for ensuring continuity of care were felt by users themselves. Many require a range of help on discharge – social care, health care or equipment. Social and health care need good co-ordination, and equipment needs to be put in place in a timely way. The user survey found that 53 per cent (n = 203) said that they needed new equipment at home after their stroke care in hospital, but the majority reported that it was not available at home on discharge. Only just over one-fifth reported that on arrival back home all of the equipment was in place. Nearly one-half reported that none was. The delivery of equipment to users who had received their rehabilitation in a stroke unit was significantly better [**EXHIBIT 27**], suggesting that the better management and co-ordination in these services resulted in improved continuity of care.

EXHIBIT 27

Users' views on the availability of equipment at home on discharge

The delivery of equipment to users who had received rehabilitation in a stroke unit was significantly better.

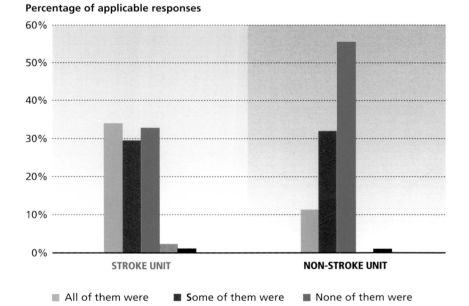

Q7 When you came home were the new things, like bath seats or new taps, already there?

Percentage of applicable responses

STROKE UNIT   NON-STROKE UNIT

- All of them were   ▪ Some of them were   ▪ None of them were
- I don't know   ▪ No response

Source: Audit Commission user survey

81. Continuity of care depends on the availability of day and community-based services to complete rehabilitation, and to monitor and review progress. The lack of these services in many areas has already been described. Just under one-half (44 per cent) of users reported never going to outpatients or to a day hospital and well over one-half (59 per cent) never received therapy at home on discharge. For those who were able to access these services, over 70 per cent reported that access was soon enough after discharge, implying good continuity of care.

82. One approach that helps to achieve better continuity is the development of protocols. Another approach is to provide ongoing outreach services that link to earlier services. A third approach is to 'inreach'. In Sheffield, the multidisciplinary community rehabilitation teams (CRTs) described in Case Study 5 recruited two community rehabilitation liaison nurses who ensure the timely, appropriate and effective assessment and transfer of patients requiring the services of the CRT. They achieve this by:

- providing 'inreach' into the hospital, assessing clients with the ward-based teams and then facilitating their transfer to the community;

- liaising with other community-based services and social services;

- ensuring accurate information is communicated between hospital and community staff;

- informing medical, nursing and therapy staff about the role and function of CRTs; and

- providing ongoing support to patients and their families being discharged to the CRTs, while in hospital, and when at home.

83. Finally, a fourth mechanism that can facilitate continuity of care is a 'key worker' system. Key worker systems are particularly useful in the management of patients in the community, where patients are located away from the team itself but where good communication and co-ordination is essential. The North Devon Re-ablement Team sees its key worker system as essential to the successful operation of the team [CASE STUDY 9, overleaf].

CASE STUDY 9

North Devon Re-ablement Team – key worker system

The operation of a key worker system is essential to the successful operation of the team. The key worker:

- is the named member of the team for client and carer to contact;

- sets therapy goals with patient/carer participation;

- ensures team members who need to be involved are kept informed of any changes;

- reports to team meetings on progress and is responsible for liaising with any other services involved;

- liaises with housing departments when needed;

- liaises with the primary care team and other community services;

- liaises with the hospital team; and

- plans discharge from the service and measures the outcomes of any intervention.

Organising and delivering care

84. Good organisation is essential if the effectiveness of rehabilitation is to be maximised. This requires above all good team work between professionals.

Team work

85. The process of rehabilitation has been described as 'continuous and multifactorial... dependent on multiple inputs' (Ref. 37). Rehabilitation requires 'a range of competencies and expertise not available from any one member of the team' (Ref. 38). Different professions, often from different organisations, need to work together. Effective team working is essential to good outcomes.

86. Team working, particularly in multidisciplinary teams, can be seen as a way of tackling the 'potential fragmentation of care; a means to widen skills; an essential part of the complexity of modern care; and a way to improve quality for the patient' (Ref. 39). However, while all teams are groups, not all groups are teams. Teams form, or are formed, to work towards a common purpose. Essential to this are clear objectives, interdependence, effective communication and clearly defined roles. This, in turn, requires effective leadership. Teams need to link into management structures. However, one of the greatest barriers to effective team working is the organisational context.

87. Effective team working and communication are difficult. Research has shown less than one in four health care teams are building effective communication and team working practices (Ref. 40).

88. Some have argued that team working costs more because of the additional costs of meeting together. However, not meeting together incurs costs through duplication of effort caused by multiple overlapping assessments and communication failures between specialties and sectors. Effective teams also save costs in other ways, such as shared files and notes. Unfortunately, many teams do not appear to be maximising their potential to co-ordinate care better.

89. All of the sites visited had an inpatient multidisciplinary team working with older people and with their rehabilitation, but only two teams used a single collaborative set of case notes and only one team prepared a single plan. In most cases, team members continued to use their own professional notes, often kept separately, and each member of the team prepared and worked to their own plan, although hopefully after discussing and sharing it with other members of the team.

Many teams do not appear to be maximising their potential to co-ordinate care.

90. There often appeared to be confusion about what constitutes a 'team'. A recent survey of community rehabilitation teams had to exclude just under one-quarter of the returns because the community rehabilitation 'team' turned out to be an individual worker (Ref. 27). The same survey found particular problems with the management of such teams. Just under one in ten of teams 'were unable to give a satisfactory and clear explanation of how their team was managed'. In one in ten teams, management was provided by a 'distant absent manager'. In one-quarter, there was no 'team' manager – instead separate heads of services managed each member. In effect nearly one-half of teams were without 'team' management. Only just over one-quarter of teams had a clear arrangement, with a team manager to whom the whole team was accountable for clinical and non-clinical matters. The same survey reported that the majority of teams did not use any regular assessment or outcome measures to monitor and review what they did and what they achieved.

91. Nevertheless, there are examples of serious efforts to improve multidisciplinary working. The North Devon Re-ablement Service described in Case Studies 6 and 9 provides professional assessment followed by a rehabilitation programme in people's own homes with goals agreed between the patient and the team. While the teams are based in hospital, allowing some inreach work, the vast majority of activity takes place in people's own homes. Liaison with all other services (for example, district nursing) and the primary care team is very important [CASE STUDY 10]. In summary, the main features of the model of multidisciplinary team working are:

- comprehensive multidisciplinary membership;
- team management through a single team manager;
- regular case meetings (weekly) and team meetings (every six weeks);
- shared multidisciplinary case notes;
- a key worker allocated to each case to co-ordinate care;
- assessments carried out according to agreed protocols;
- goals agreed with the patient and/or carer – they receive a copy of the care plan;
- protocols developed for sharing information – free flow of information and good communication is essential to team working;
- review and discharge dates set according to protocol arrangements; and
- data collected to aid service evaluation.

92. Another example – this time of a team working together well in a hospital – is the Bradford Stroke Unit [CASE STUDY 11, overleaf]. Prior to the establishment of the unit, stroke patients in Bradford were scattered across many different wards. The establishment of the unit has allowed multidisciplinary working to develop much more fully. The overall length of stay has reduced to an average of 31 days. The unit has a policy of admitting patients of any age or circumstance if conscious, yet it still achieves a rate of return home of nearly 60 per cent.

CASE STUDY 10

North Devon Re-ablement Service – team work

- The service is **multidisciplinary**. Members include: manager, co-ordinator (admin/clerical), nurse, physiotherapist, OT, speech and language therapists (SaLT), support workers, medical sessions and social workers. There is also access to psychologist input.

- There **is a team manager** and team members report to the manager. The lines of accountability are clear. (They get professional support by keeping a reporting line to their professional heads). There is time for communication between team members. Flexibility is seen as essential. Support workers will do what is required through flexible working.

- The team **meets weekly** for allocation and review and **every six weeks** for a broader team planning meeting. Everyone attends including the doctor.

- At the point of referral, multidisciplinary case notes are created (and with greater social services input these are to become multi-agency too). The team operates a **shared file** system. Background information is collected only once. Colour coded sections are then completed by the relevant disciplines. There is also a team communication record (patients can complete this too). Patient-held records are maintained throughout.

- Appropriate referrals normally go to the weekly allocation meeting, but urgent referrals are responded to within two days. Each referral is allocated a **key worker** to co-ordinate their treatment plan.

- Core information is gathered using agreed **assessment protocols**. Carers are asked if they want an assessment of their own needs.

- **Goals are agreed with the patient and/or carer.** A re-ablement plan incorporating patient goals and care is agreed. Individuals receive copies of their care plan.

- The person making the initial face-to-face contact introduces the service and leaves **information** about the services and a communication record.

- After initial contact, a **review** date is set. At this, either another review date or a discharge is planned. Contact is maintained with relevant services throughout – for example, GP, primary health care team, SSD. Wherever possible, team members attend local primary care groups.

- Service **performance evaluation** is measured using baseline data on patient characteristics, referral source, length of stay and outcome. Client and carer satisfaction is monitored.

Bradford Stroke Unit

Prior to the establishment of the stroke unit, patients in Bradford were scattered across many wards at St Lukes and Bradford Royal Infirmary. An audit in 1995 showed stroke patients present on 15 wards. In October 1997, the stroke unit was established with 21 beds.

The policy is to admit patients of any age if conscious. Patients are identified by 'liaison nurses' who 'case find' and carry out pre-transfer assessments according to an agreed protocol. Once on the stroke unit, the multidisciplinary team provides care. Membership comprises: social services staff, SLTs, physiotherapists, nursing staff, therapy assistants, physicians, and stroke outreach staff. Generic therapy assistants provide support to all therapy disciplines. A specific training programme has been developed. The staff work under the close supervision of the lead therapist and usefully extend the therapy day to weekends.

Being a designated unit allows a clear patient focus with a common purpose. Other approaches aid team working, co-ordination and ensure continuity of care. These are:

- **smaller sub-teams** – three smaller teams, each focused on seven beds, provide a highly individualised rehabilitation focus to seven patients. This allows one-to-one psychological support that is a vital aspect of stroke recovery and adjustment;

- **goal planning** – each patient is reviewed weekly by the team to discuss progress and to plan multidisciplinary short- and medium-term rehabilitation goals with dates of expected achievement. The unit is experimenting with patients and carers attending the meeting to maximise their involvement;

- **full team meetings** – are held weekly and involve community and social services staff;

- **collaborative case notes** – these are used to support team working by sharing assessments, progress and information;

- **interdisciplinary training** – the unit developed an in-house interdisciplinary training programme that has been evaluated by an externally funded research project. This demonstrated that the programme achieved measurable improvements in care;

- **education** – a weekly multidisciplinary teaching session is held at which all staff on the unit take turns to present a pre-arranged stroke topic. External speakers are also invited;

- **audit** – the unit participates in the Royal College of Physicians national stroke audit and has also established an ongoing audit based on a validated patient satisfaction questionnaire sent to all patients after discharge;

- **patient information** – the unit has developed its own 'easy guide' to help patients and their families to better understand stroke. A stroke information pack is also provided around the time of discharge. A telephone helpline has been established for carers and ex-patients of the unit.

- the **overall length of stay** has shortened to an average of 31 days in the Stroke Unit and the overall time spent in hospital is 43 days. The unit takes all strokes but still achieves a return home rate of nearly 60 per cent. Around 30 per cent enter long-stay care (two-thirds of these enter nursing homes); and

- **continued care** – is available through a stroke-specific outreach physiotherapist who attends team meetings and through a neurology outpatient clinic.

Stroke care

93. There is strong evidence, according to the *Stroke Unit Trialists' Collaboration*, that organised stroke care (provided by a multidisciplinary team in a stroke unit) reduces mortality and improves outcomes (lower institutionalisation rates) significantly (Ref. 20). There is sufficient evidence to support the setting up of well-organised stroke services. Care provided by a multidisciplinary team on a stroke unit achieves a better patient outcome than care provided on a general medical ward.

'The evidence indicates that these services should provide comprehensive care centred on an integrated multidisciplinary team who have a specialist interest in stroke rehabilitation. A team is a group of individuals who share common values and work towards common goals. Such teams usually work in a geographically defined stroke unit. Sometimes teams care for stroke patients throughout a hospital without a defined unit. Features distinguishing such services from general medical services are: co-ordinated interdisciplinary care, involvement of family and carers in the rehabilitation process, specialisation, and education of staff, patients and carers' (Ref. 20).

...much stroke care and rehabilitation remains fragmented and disorganised.

94. Despite the evidence, much stroke care and rehabilitation remains fragmented and disorganised. As far back as 1988, a conference at the King's Fund Centre (Ref. 41) concluded that stroke services that are provided in hospital, primary care, and the community seemed haphazard, fragmented and poorly tailored to the patient's needs. In 1998, the Clinical Standards Advisory Group also found that standards of service varied widely around the country, and that practice was often poor (Ref. 42). Out of 20 trusts, 13 had a designated stroke service, of which 9 could properly be called stroke units. A Stroke Association survey, published in 1999, found that only one-half of stroke patients received optimal specialist stroke services on a stroke unit or through a stroke team (Ref. 43). Finally, the National Sentinel Audit of Stroke, published in December 1999, found that less than one-half of all trusts participating had stroke units (Ref. 44). Only 18 per cent of patients spent more than one-half of their stay on stroke units, 15 per cent on rehabilitation units and 67 per cent on general medical wards. However, their findings confirmed that patients received better care within stroke units. They also specifically reported that care in stroke units was significantly better than that in general rehabilitation units as well as that on general medical wards. They found that many aspects of care did not meet basic standards.

95. Audit Commission findings are very much in line with these results: dedicated stroke beds (a stroke unit) were accessible to people aged 75 and over in only one-half of localities, and the number of beds available for rehabilitation varied nearly fivefold. Of the 16 study sites, 11 had a 'lead' consultant and a dedicated multidisciplinary team working on stroke rehabilitation, but none worked with all cases including 'outliers' placed elsewhere. In five, no multidisciplinary team was dedicated to stroke rehabilitation, despite the needs and proven benefits.

96. The management of 'outliers' is important. Although a stroke unit, or designated beds may exist, capacity is inevitably limited, and some patients receive their rehabilitation elsewhere. Such patients do not receive the full benefits of care provided by the trained multidisciplinary team working with stroke patients. In 6 hospitals studied in detail, widely varying proportions of patients aged 75 and over with a stroke were still on acute wards 21 days after admission [**EXHIBIT 28**]. Significant proportions of stroke patients in all six hospitals never gained access to either a stroke unit or a rehabilitation ward [**EXHIBIT 29**].

EXHIBIT 28

Percentage of stroke patients aged 75 and over on acute wards 21 days after admission

A large proportion of patients are still located on the acute wards in some locations.

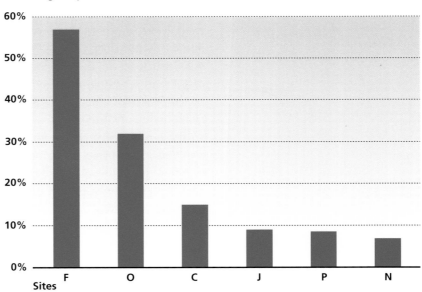

Percentage of patients

Source: Audit Commission stroke case analysis

EXHIBIT 29

Patient locations – completed stays

In some locations, a majority of patients aged 75 and over do not gain access to a stroke unit or rehabilitation ward.

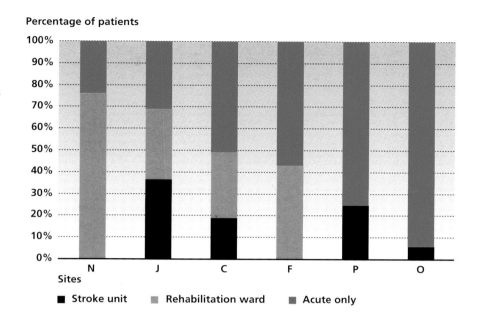

Percentage of patients

Sites: N, J, C, F, P, O

■ Stroke unit ■ Rehabilitation ward ■ Acute only

Source: Audit Commission stroke case analysis

Conclusion

97. Taken together, the picture is one of disorganised rather than organised care. Certainly, the management and organisation of care is much less than is needed to reap the full potential benefits. The authors of the National Sentinel Audit for Stroke note that collecting stroke 'patients together in a stroke unit should lead to improved efficiency, rather than greater costs'. Also, at ward level, the development of protocols for managing common stroke complications, improving communication through regular meetings and sharing notes, and involving patients and carers in the planning of care are all achievable without much financial investment. The clinical and cost evidence is such that no one should be denied access to organised stroke care, and the benefits of multidisciplinary assessment and rehabilitation should be available to all older people who could benefit.

RECOMMENDATIONS

3 Managing the Rehabilitation Programme

Rehabilitation programmes need to be better managed:

1 Agencies ought to be considering their screening arrangements and developing assessment procedures together that review people's potential for rehabilitation.

2 Good communication is essential for success: people need to become fully and positively engaged in their own rehabilitation programmes, which can often be difficult and painful.

3 Extra care is needed when people transfer between services and organisations.

4 Good team working is important, with multidisciplinary and multi-agency teams working to a single manager and with protocols setting out what is required when people are moved on to receive other services.

5 Organised stroke care should be available to all who could benefit.

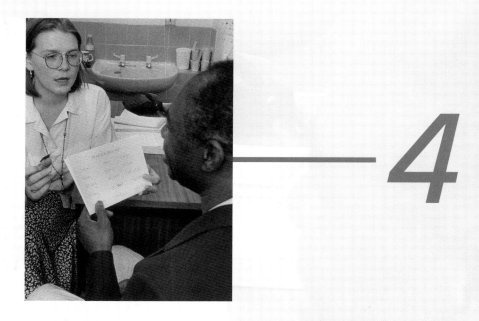

4

Therapists and Rehabilitation Services

Therapists are key members of any multidisciplinary
rehabilitation team. More are needed, requiring better
long-term workforce planning. In the short term, the level
of therapy can be increased by using therapy assistants and
using qualified therapists more flexibly.

98. Therapists play a crucial role in the delivery of rehabilitation services. They are important members of teams and are central to assessment, the setting of goals and the provision of care and services. Recently, they have been coming under increasing pressure. The numbers of initial contacts (new referrals) have been increasing steadily over the last ten years [EXHIBIT 30]. If authorities and trusts are to deliver rehabilitation programmes successfully, they must manage this key resource with care, and that is the subject of this chapter. Therapists do more than rehabilitation. While this report focuses on their contribution to rehabilitation, this chapter touches upon issues of wider relevance.

99. Despite the growth in the numbers of therapists, there remain genuine difficulties in meeting demand in many areas. If scarce therapy time is to be used to best effect, it must be matched to demand carefully. Measuring demand is therefore the first step in an effective management programme. An accurate picture of demand requires information about how many people are referred, how many times they are seen, and who sees them, which in turn depends on the complexity of their needs, or 'casemix'.

100. Physiotherapy and occupational therapy departments make annual 'Korner' returns to the DoH, that record how many people are seen (the total number of initial contacts) by age and source of referral. For occupational therapy, additional information is collected on how many times people are seen and where they are seen. Apart from 'Korner' data, departments collect other information about demand, but to very varying degrees. Two sites were using 'physiotherapy input units' (PIUs) that are

EXHIBIT 30

Therapist initial contacts as a percentage of 1988/99 level

Initial contacts with therapists have increased considerably over the last ten years.

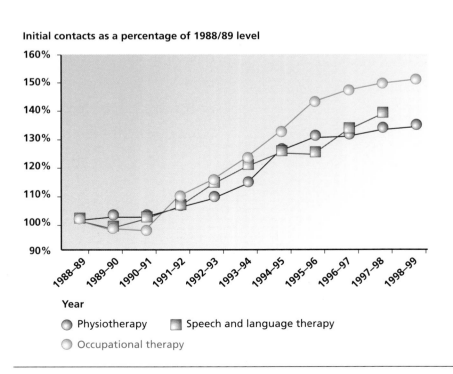

Initial contacts as a percentage of 1988/89 level

Source: DoH data

simple input measures that take casemix into account [**BOX D**]. Stockport Hospital NHS Trust physiotherapy department was using PIUs and the department manager found them useful in monitoring and moving staff between specialties to areas of greatest need [**CASE STUDY 12**].

BOX D

Physiotherapy input units (PIUs)

Weighted contacts:

Students	x 0.63
Assistant	x 0.35
Staff grade/basic grade	x 0.63
Senior II:	x 0.8
Senior I:	x 1
Superintendent:	x 1

Source: Joyce Williams (Ref.45)

PIUs are a useful and simple way of measuring comparative demand on departments. For each patient, total contacts are recorded, along with the grade of staff carrying out the contacts. Each contact is weighted, according to the staff grade involved in therapy.

When aggregated over a service, the total (contacts x weighting) is a measure of demand that goes beyond the crude 'contact'. It reflects the complexity of the cases handled, by assuming that more complex patients will require higher grade staff time. Patients in services can be 'banded' according to how many PIUs they have received. As such, PIUs are helpful for monitoring and contracting purposes: year-on-year comparisons can be made for a service. Also, weightings are based loosely on salary differentials, and can reflect the approximate cost of episodes of care.

However, the system assumes that the person carrying out the contact is the most appropriate person to do so, when in fact this may be more dependent on who is available. It also assumes that each patient has a sufficient number of contacts, when this too may also be affected by staff availability.

Modified PIUs can also be used in occupational therapy.

CASE STUDY 12

Stockport Hospitals NHS Trust physiotherapy department – use of therapy input units to link casemix and staff time

Stockport Hospitals NHS Trust physiotherapy department uses PIUs to monitor the input given to patients at ward level.

PIUs are used to record the physiotherapy inputs that can be related directly to named patients, including patient-related administration and direct contact time. A PIU is equivalent to ten minutes of helper time; other grades use a multiple of this unit to reflect their skill level, based on salary ratios.

Patients are allocated retrospectively into one of seven bands given different case weightings, depending on how many PIUs they receive. This information is aggregated at a ward and a specialty level, to monitor trends in the severity of cases passing through the ward or specialty.

The department manager has also used PIUs to calculate the cost of contacts with GPs.

*...different priority...
is... accorded to the
funding of therapy posts
in different parts of the
country.*

101. The system for agreeing service levels for therapy does not encourage better demand information. Therapy is usually part of a block contract and normally service levels are set around 'initial contacts per year'. Therapy services are listed as an 'overhead' on NHS trust financial returns. Therapy staffing levels have largely been set on an historical basis, based upon previous levels. Only two sites visited had attempted to set staffing levels in relation to any assessment of workload. In both these cases, the link between staffing and workload had been made for small, specific services rather than the whole department. In this context of poor information, poor commissioning, and staffing levels rolled forward each year, it is not surprising that the availability of therapists varies widely from locality to locality. For physiotherapy, data on the level of staffing in different localities show that the area with the highest staffing has 8 times more therapist time available per 100,000 population than the lowest. For occupational therapy the difference was **threefold**, while for speech and language therapy the difference was **sevenfold**. This variation shows the different priority accorded to the funding of therapy posts in different parts of the country, probably because of a lack of appreciation of the contribution they make to care.

102. Another problem is that national shortages make it difficult for some areas to improve the situation. Nationally, there are difficulties with recruiting and retaining staff, particularly 'hands-on' qualified staff. For physiotherapists, data from 48 trusts show that the staff in post as a percentage of established posts was lowest for the qualified grades (senior 1 and 2), and was highest for managers and assistants [**EXHIBIT 31**]. For speech and language therapists, the pattern was similar, with staff in post as a percentage of established posts lowest for the qualified grades, and highest for managers and assistants [**EXHIBIT 32, overleaf**]. The pattern was different for occupational therapy. Manager posts were furthest from establishment, but there were also significant deficits in qualified posts, especially senior 2s [**EXHIBIT 33, overleaf**].

103. These figures show the average staffing against establishment levels across 48 NHS trusts. The range between trusts is wide. For example, physiotherapy staff in post as a percentage of established staff for senior 2 grade posts is only just over 30 per cent in the worst case [**EXHIBIT 34, overleaf**], and only 8 trusts are staffed at or above establishment levels. For occupational therapy, the staff in post as a percentage of established staff for senior grade 2 posts is under 20 per cent in the worst case but over 50 per cent of trusts are staffed at or above establishment [**EXHIBIT 35, overleaf**]. Trusts occasionally recruit above establishment levels, on the rare occasions where more than enough suitable candidates apply for posts, grabbing qualified staff when they can get them.

104. Staff shortages affect patients. The user survey found that while over one-half of stroke patients were satisfied with the amount of therapy they received, nearly one-third felt that contact was 'not often enough' [**EXHIBIT 36, overleaf**].

CASE STUDY 14

Bradford – improvements in amputation rehabilitation

This was an interdisciplinary project to improve the rehabilitation of patients requiring lower limb amputation. There was concern that inpatient stays were long and that patients had limited access to therapy activities, inhibiting the restoration of function. Although focused initially on a specific group of patients, it was hoped that the model, if successful, could be transferable to other areas within the Trust.

Recognising the benefits that could accrue from better multidisciplinary working in terms of improved functional outcomes through improved communication and support, the project aimed to:

- develop effective interdisciplinary working by improving communication across the team;

- improve the quality of care for patients by increasing the amount of active rehabilitation and creating an environment to maximise patient activity and independence;

- evaluate the impact of the generic therapy assistant role in increasing therapeutic activity;

- improve patient information; and

- reduce the overall length of stay and improve the discharge processes.

Organisational changes were introduced in order to try and achieve these aims. These changes included:

- a six bedded bay allocated primarily for patients requiring amputee rehabilitation;

- improved multidisciplinary team arrangements. Weekly meetings were introduced to discuss and review patient goals. A social worker was designated for this group of patients, helping to highlight and address factors affecting discharge. Daily team updates were introduced focusing on the care plans that had been developed;

- generic therapy assistants were introduced, employed on a seven-day week basis to increase the therapeutic activity undertaken by patients. They received competency based training in physiotherapy, occupational therapy and nursing skills relating to amputees;

- therapy assistants were focused on reducing solitary behaviour, increasing camaraderie, motivation, independence and a patient's belief in his/her ability to recover. The bay was equipped with rehabilitation equipment and drink-making facilities to encourage early independence; and

- an information pack was introduced for patients.

Evaluation showed that a number of significant benefits and improvements flowed from these changes:

Demographic data relating to patients treated during the retrospective year prior to the project were similar in terms of the average age and sex distribution to the group treated under the new arrangements. Average age was 71.45 years for the retrospective group and 71.31 years for the prospective group. But, average length of stay was reduced by 32 per cent, from 43.39 days to 25.48 days. All patients returned to independent living. Observation of a random population of patients showed that the prospective group was spending 39 per cent as opposed to 5 per cent of observational periods for the retrospective group in useful therapeutic activity. The time spent in interactive behaviour doubled.

The Trust concluded that greater resources for a fuller evaluation would be welcome as the information collected suggested that a low-cost approach to changes in the organisation and delivery of rehabilitation is effective. Projects have been introduced to test the transferability of the therapy assistant concept to other specialties, including orthopaedics and stroke.

Improving flexibility

113. Greater flexibility and a more innovative approach could help therapists to improve their contribution to rehabilitation services. They could also play a significant part in helping to address issues to do with demand management across both health and social care.

114. Within acute services, too often the role of the OT is limited to 'discharge facilitation' or 'safe discharge'. A more flexible use of therapists by trusts can help to reduce hospital admissions for those who genuinely do not require them. At the Princess Royal Hospital, Haywards Heath, the deployment of an OT within an accident and emergency unit helped to manage admissions to hospital of older people, and improved the quality of care given by providing advice, liaison, the provision of equipment and follow-up at home [CASE STUDY 15].

CASE STUDY 15

The Princess Royal Hospital, Haywards Heath, West Sussex – occupational therapy within A&E

An OT was placed in the accident and emergency department and medical assessment unit for a trial six week period. The aim was to provide objective information on the functional abilities of a patient to assist in deciding whether the patient needed to be admitted to a hospital ward or discharged.

Nearly 92 per cent of referrals came from A&E and just over 83 per cent of these were patients who had fallen, with or without fracture(s). Following OT assessment, under 30 per cent were admitted. Just under 80 per cent were aged 75 or over.

The OT interventions included:

- functional assessments – particularly of transfers and mobility;

- advice – for example, dressing techniques and the availability of community services;

- liaison with patient/family/ carers for background information;

- liaison with and referrals to district nurses and social services for overnight visits, home care and the provision of equipment;

- the provision of equipment for discharge; and

- home visits following discharge on the same day or following day – to provide further advice/equipment/support to maintain safety and independence.

The average time spent with patients admitted was 1.75 hours and for patients discharged it was 3.5 hours.

Data for the six week period prior to the pilot were compared with data for the pilot itself (table below). When looking specifically at people aged 75 years or over, the percentage of elderly patients admitted to wards following assessment and treatment in A&E reduced by 10 per cent during the project period.

A&E admissions age 75 or over

	Six weeks before pilot 21 January 1998–3 March 1998	Six weeks pilot 4 March 1998–15 April 1998
A&E admissions	274	308
A&E onto hospital ward	105 (36.7 per cent)	85 (27.6 per cent)

115. In Victoria in London, a joint health and social care project has been set up to increase the levels of community-based occupational therapy to people aged 65 or over [CASE STUDY 16]. The project arose from concerns that, too often, patients left hospital without any plan for follow-up support in the community, resulting in some having to be re-admitted. Through focused assessment and care management, care costs have been minimised by promoting independence and not encouraging dependence. Savings have also been made in the provision of equipment through more effective assessment, practical problem-solving and good follow up. The project team also identified that increased use of assistants, provided there was commitment to appropriate training, could increase savings and ensure that qualified therapists were correctly used.

CASE STUDY 16

Victoria Project, London – enhanced community occupational therapy (Ref. 48)

The 'Victoria Project' (run by Riverside Community Health Care) was funded with a £50,000 grant by the King's Fund to the Kensington, Chelsea and Westminster Commissioning Agency and Westminster Social Services. It was set up to explore how services could be purchased more effectively to meet the needs of elderly people in the Victoria district of London. The project provided a community assessment and rehabilitation service for people aged 65 and over. Service elements included:

- the assessment of functional ability;
- the rehabilitation to improve or maintain functional ability for up to three months;
- the provision of aids and minor adaptations to maximise independence within the home;
- the reduction of inappropriate or unnecessary dependency on services and carers;
- the introduction of a care management role, to ensure effective communication and referral onto appropriate agencies; and
- the provision of advisory and liaison service for other people working with the client group.

The team was also asked to evaluate the effectiveness of occupational therapy intervention and to provide a 'blueprint' for future patterns of care.

The evaluated impact of the project has shown that:

- there has been a substantial reduction in domiciliary care with subsequent savings to social services of over £65,000 per annum; and
- further savings on reduced equipment provision of £14,250 per annum.

116. Within social services, the role of the OT may be limited to the assessment for, and provision of, equipment and adaptations to people's homes. This role fails to make full use of their skills. They can make a significant contribution to the assessment of older people at risk of entering long-term care, or in receipt of high-cost packages of care. Nottingham Social Services Department has begun to deploy its OTs in a much more creative way [CASE STUDY 17]. They are helping to manage down the level of home-care packages and the number of long-term placements in residential and nursing homes.

117. Taken together, evidence shows that a more flexible deployment of therapists, particularly OTs as part of a multidisciplinary approach, can make a significant contribution to help manage demand across health and social care, and improve outcomes and the quality of life of older people.

CASE STUDY 17

Nottingham – The strategic use of occupational therapy

Nottingham City Social Services Department has reviewed the impact of occupational therapy skills within the framework of assessment and care management and home-care teams. The review uncovered potential savings to SSDs through more creative use of scarce occupational therapy resources.

The project began with an OT assessing the dependency levels of service users who were receiving home care five to seven days a week. Using a standardised dependency index, of those assessed (n =56) just over one-half were found to have the potential to be more independent. The review found that:

- some people discharged from hospital still had intensive packages many months later, suggesting the need for structured reviews; and
- home-care staff were performing tasks for people that they could do themselves, wasting resources and prolonging dependency.

This led to the OT reviewing selected home-care packages where there had been requests for more support. Out of 46 reviews, only 1 received an increase in service, with 10 having a reduced service and 6 having the service withdrawn.

During the same period, 21 people were referred for long-term placement in residential/nursing home care. Joint visits were made with social work staff and an OT assessment was completed. As a result, 12 people were kept in their own home, 8 of whom received OT support.

The review of the project concluded that a more creative use of community OTs by social services can lead to more effective and cost-efficient community care services and can help to ensure that expensive home-care packages and long-term care placements are only used for people who really need them.

The use of new 'financial flexibilities'

131. The need for greater financial flexibility has also been recognised and has been assisted by new legislation. Arrangements that allow closer working are being strengthened following the consultation papers *Partnership in Action* (Ref. 10) in England and *Partnership for Improvement* (Ref. 11) in Wales. These papers set out the basis for shared health and social services arrangements, including the relaxation of rules about funding for health and social care. Until now, health and social services have been unable to pool their resources to any significant extent, hindering the development of integrated services. The *NHS Act 1999* (Ref. 12) now allows pooled funds, 'lead commissioning' and integrated provision. For rehabilitation services, which are funded and provided across agencies, these new arrangements could make a significant contribution to better co-ordinated care.

132. The new arrangements provide a real opportunity to ensure closer working between professionals delivering rehabilitation services through a better framework of joint working. The creation of community older people's teams, complete with physicians, nurses, therapists, social care staff, etc could be one way to provide better integrated and linked services, provided a suitable system of governance can be devised. One possibility is a joint team under a single manager who holds the pooled budget and who reports upwards to a board made up of representatives from each agency contributing funds. Such a model would have an 'hourglass' structure [**EXHIBIT 43**].

EXHIBIT 43

Governance arrangements for joint teams

One possibility is a joint team under a single manager who holds the pooled budget.

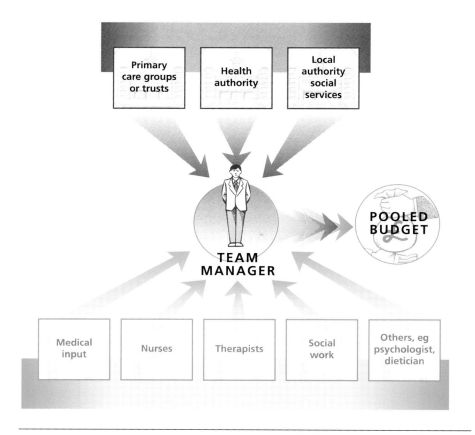

Source: Audit Commission

133. Such a team could also eventually work across agencies and settings, replacing the model of Exhibit 2 with a new model linking services more closely, with the integrated joint re-ablement team moving to the centre [EXHIBIT 44].

EXHIBIT 44

A new model for linking services more closely

The integrated joint re-ablement team would move to the centre.

Source: Audit Commission

References

1. Audit Commission, *Forget Me Not: Mental Health Services for Older People*, Audit Commission, 1999.

2. Audit Commission, *Fully Equipped: The Provision of Equipment to Older or Disabled People by the NHS and Social Services in England and Wales*, Audit Commission, 2000.

3. Audit Commission, *Charging with Care: How Councils Charge for Home Care*, Audit Commission, 2000.

4. Audit Commission, *The Coming of Age: Improving Care Services for Older People*, Audit Commission, 1997.

5. A Report by The Royal Commission on Long Term Care, *With Respect to Old Age: Long Term Care – Rights and Responsibilities*, The Stationery Office, 1999.

6. J Young, 'Rehabilitation and Older People', *British Medical Journal*, Vol. 313, p677.

7. Audit Commission, *United They Stand: Co-ordinating Care for Elderly Patients with Hip Fracture*, Audit Commission HMSO, 1995.

8. Department of Health, Executive Letter EL(97)62, *Better Services for Vulnerable People*, October 1997.

9. Department of Health, *Better Services for Vulnerable People – Maintaining the Momentum*, Letter from NHS Executive, August 1998.

10. Department of Health, *Partnership in Action*, NHS Executive, 1998.

11. Welsh Office, *Partnership for Improvement*, Welsh Office, 1998.

12. Department of Health, *National Health Services Act 1999*, Department of Health, 1999.

13. Department of Health, *Modernising Health and Social Services: National Priorities Guidance 1999/00–2001/02*, Department of Health, 1998.

14. National Assembly for Wales, *A Better Wales*, National Assembly for Wales, 1999.

15. Department of Health, *Modernising Social Services*, Department of Health, 1999.

16. A Nocon and S Baldwin, *Trends in Rehabilitation Policy – A Literature Review*, London, King's Fund, 1998.

17. E Dickinson and A Sinclair, *Effective Practice in Rehabilitation – Reviewing the Evidence*, London, King's Fund 1998.

18. Royal College of Physicians, London, *Ensuring Equity and Quality of Care for Elderly People*, Royal College of Physicians, London, 1994.

19. C Wolfe, T Rudd and R Beech (eds), *Stroke Services and Research: An Overview with Recommendations for Future Research*. The Stroke Association, London, 1996.

20. Stroke Unit Trialists' Collaboration. 'Collaborative systematic review of the randomised trials of organised inpatient (stroke unit) care after stroke', *British Medical Journal*, 1997; 314: pp1151–9.

21. Royal College of Nursing, *Rehabilitating Older People: The Role of the Nurse*, Royal College of Nursing, London, March 2000.

22. S Younger-Ross, T Lomax and T Outlands, 'Five years on', *Community Care Management*, Vol. 6, 1, 1998.

23. Devon Social Services, *The Exebank Handbook, Exebank Rehabilitation Unit*, Exmouth, Devon, 1999.

24. Social Services Inspectorate, South and West, *Rehabilitation Workshop*, Social Services Inspectorate, 1998.

25. D Sanderson and D Wright, *Final Evaluation of the CARATs Initiatives in Rotherham*, YHEC, University of York, 1999.

26. G Herbert and J Townsend, *Rehabilitation Pathways for Older People*, Draft Summary Report, Nuffield Institute for Health, University of Leeds and YHEC, University of York.

27. P Enderby, *A Survey of Community Rehabilitation in the United Kingdom*, University of Sheffield, November 1999.

28. S Sanderson, S Hummel and N Edwards, *Assessment of Inpatient and other Facilities in General Medicine and Medicine for the Elderly*, Report for Rotherham General Hospitals NHS Trust, YHEC, University of York; 1996.

29. J Robinson and S Turnock, *Investing in Rehabilitation*, London, King's Fund, 1998.

30. A Stuck, et al, 'Comprehensive geriatric assessment: a meta-analysis of controlled trials', *The Lancet*, Vol. 343, p1032, 1993.

31. Department of Geriatric Medicine, St George's Hospital Medical School, *Nursing Home Placements For Older People in England and Wales: A National Audit 1995–1998*, St George's Hospital Medical School, London, February 1999.

32. K Stewart, D Challis, I Carpenter, E Dickinson, 'Assessment approaches for older people receiving social care: content and coverage', *Journal of Geriatic Physchiatry*, Vol. 14, pp147–56.

33. J Stevenson, *Comprehensive Assessment of Older People*, King's Fund Rehabilitation Programme Developing Rehabilitation Opportunities for Older People, Briefing Paper 2, 1999.

34. College of Occupational Therapy, *Code of Ethics and Professional Conduct*, College of Occupational Therapy, 1995.

35. College of Occupational Therapy, *The Therapeutic Intervention by OTs with Consumers in Their Own Homes*, College of Occupational Therapy, 1993.

36. Chartered Society of Physiotherapy, *Standards of Physiotherapy Practice, Standard 23*, Chartered Society of Physiotherapy.

37. AJ Squires, 'Key issues for purchasers and providers in hospital, day hospital and community rehabilitation services for older people', in *A Unique Window of Change*, NHS Health Advisory Service, Annual Report 1992–93, HMSO, London.

38. M Hastings, *Teamworking in Rehabilitation* in A Squires, (ed), *Rehabilitation of Older People – A Handbook for the Multidisciplinary Team*, Chapman and Hall, 1996.

39. J Firth-Cozens, 'Celebrating teamwork', *Quality in Healthcare*, Vol. 7 Supplement, December 1998.

40. M West, 'Communication and teamworking in healthcare', *NT Research*, Vol. 4, No. 1, 1999.

41. King's Fund Consensus Statement, 'The treatment of stroke', *British Medical Journal*, 1988, 297: pp126–8.

42. Clinical Standards Advisory Group, *Report on Clinical Effectiveness Using Stroke Care as an Example*, London, Stationery Office, 1998.

43. S Ebrahim and J Redfern, *Stroke Care – A Matter of Chance: A National Survey of Stroke Services*, The Stroke Association, London, 1999.

44. A G Rudd, P Irwin, Z Rutledge, D Lowe, D Wade, R Morris and MG Pearson, 'The national sentinel audit for stroke: a tool for raising standards of care', *Journal of the Royal College of Physicians of London*, Vol. 33, 5, September/October 1999.

45. J Williiams, *Calculating Staffing Levels in Physiotherapy Services*, Pampas Publishing.

46. G Kwakkel, et al, 'Intensity of leg and arm training after primary middle-cerebral-artery stroke: a randomised trial', *The Lancet*, 17 July 1999.

47. D Wade, 'Rehabilitation therapy after stroke', *The Lancet*, 17 July 1999, p176.

48. Riverside Community Healthcare, *The Victoria Project: Community Occupational Therapy Rehabilitation Service – Research Findings and Recommendations*, Riverside Community Healthcare, May 1998.

49. Department of Health, *Shaping the Future of the NHS: Long Term Planning for Hospitals and Related Services*. Consultation Document on the *Findings of the National Beds Inquiry*. Department of Health, 2000.

50. D McMahon, *Intermediate Care: A Challenge to the Specialty of Geriatric Medicine or Its Renaissance?* (forthcoming).

51. Department of Health, *Statistical Bulletin*, 1998/31, Department of Health, September, 1998.

52. Department of Health, *Modernising Health and Social Services: National Priorities Guidance 2000/01–2002/03*, Department of Health, 1999.

53. Department of Health, *Burdens of Disease*, NHS Executive, 1996.

54. R Malmgren, J Bamford, C Warlow, P Sandercock and J Slattery, 'Projecting the number of patients with first-ever strokes and patients newly-handicapped by stroke in England and Wales', *British Medical Journal* 1989; 298: pp656–60.

55. N Bosanquet and P Franks, *Stroke Care: Reducing the Burden of Disease*, Stroke Association, London, 1998.

56. G Greveson and O James, 'Improving long-term outcome after stroke – the views of patients and carers', *Health Trends*, 1991; Vol. 23:4.

57. P Pound, P Gompetz and S Ebrahim, 'Patients' satisfaction with stroke services', *Clinical Rehabilitation*, 1994; Vol. 8; pp7–17.

58. M Kelson and C Ford, *Stroke Rehabiliation: Patient and Carer Views*, Royal College of Physicians of London, 1998.

59. W J Scholte op Reimer, R J de Haan, M Limburg, and G A M van des Bos, 'Patients' satisfaction with care after stroke: relation with characteristics of patients and care', *Quality in Health Care*, 1996; Vol. 5: pp144–150.

60. C Thomas and A Parry, 'Research on users' views about stroke services: towards an empowerment research paradigm or more of the same?', *Physiotherapy*, 1996; Vol. 82(1): pp6–12.

Index References are to paragraph numbers, Boxes and Case Studies (page numbers)

A

Access to services 12, 51

Accident and emergency
units Case Study 15 (p80)

Acute care 21–25, 29–30, 58, 69

Advisory group Appendix 1

Age-related conditions 2, 16, 18

Ageing population 1

Airedale NHS Trust Case Study 7 (p38)

Amputation rehabilitation
Case Study 14 (p79)

Aphasia Appendix 3

Assessment procedures 13, 71–71,
Box C (p50)

Assistant staff 109

Audit Commission
locality data Preface, 33, 50

B

Bank staff 105

Better Services For Vulnerable
People (DoH) 5, 125

Bradford
amputation rehabilitation 112;
Case Study 14 (p79);
Box F (p94)

Oaks Resource Centre 57;
Case Study 7 (p38)

Bradford Stroke Unit 92;
Case Study 11 (p60)

C

Cardio-respiratory diseases 2

Care pathways
assessment 13, 71–73
care planning 74–76
continuity of care 15, 77–84
screening 48–70

Care planning 74–76

Chichester, St Richards Hospital 111;
Case Study 13 (p78)

Chronic disease 2, 18

Clinical Standards Advisory Group 94

Co-ordinated care 10–11, 58–66, 126,
Case Study 18 (pp89–90)

Coming of Age (The) 3

Communication
in teams 87–90
to patients 74–76

Community-based services 24–25,
48–57; Case Study 6A (p35),
Case Study 6B (p36),
Case Study 7 (p38)

Victoria Project, London
Case Study 16 (p81);
Box F (p94)

Community hospitals 46; Box B (p29)

Continuity of care 15, 77–84

Cost-effectiveness
rehabilitation generally 134–140,
Box F (p94)

social services rehabilitation
schemes Case Study 1A (p23),
Case Study 2 (p26),
Case Study 3 (p27)

D

Day care centres 57,
Case Study 7 (p38)

Day hospitals 48–51, 57, 81

Delivery of care
stroke units 93–97
team work 21–25, 49, 54–56, 85–92,
Case Study 5 (p34)
Case Study 6A; 6B (pp35, 36)
Case Study 10 (p59),
Case Study 11 (p60)

Devon Social Services Department
Case Study 1A;1B (p23, p24)

Disability 2, 16–19

E

Easy Care Elderly Assessment
System Box C (p50)

Effective Practice in Rehabilitation
(Audit Commission and King's
Fund) 11, 22

Equipment 80

Exebank, Exmouth Case Study 1A, 1B
(p23, p24)

F

Femoral fractures 2
research into rehabilitation
pathways and costs Box B (p29)

Financial flexibility 131–133

Flexible staffing 113–117

Funding
financial flexibility 131–133
social services rehabilitation
schemes Case Study 1A(p23)
Case Study 2 (p26)
Case Study 3 (p27)

G

Geriatric medicine 122

Goals 75

H

Haywards Heath, Princess
Royal Hospital Case Study 15 (p80);
Box F (p94)

Health Improvement Programmes 25

Home-based rehabilitation 51

Hospital admissions 3–5, 24
inpatient rehabilitation 28–31,
Box A (p16)

I

Independence 5–9, 121–123

Inpatient rehabilitation 29–31, 58

Integrated services 6–15, 58–66,
126–130,
Case Study 18 (pp89–90)

Intermediate rehabilitation
services 24–25, 35–47,
Case Study 1A; 1B (pp23, 24)
Case Study 2 (p26)
Case Study 3 (p27); Box B (p27)

J

Joint investment plans (JIPs) 5, 125

Joint working 6–9, 124–125, 131–132

K

Keighley, Oaks Resource Centre   57;
                    Case Study 7 (p38)

Key workers   3; *Case Study 9* (p56)

L

Locality data   Preface, 33, 50

Locums   105–106

M

Minimum data sets   *Box C* (p50)

*Modernising Health and Social
    Services: National Priorities
    Guidance 1999/2000-2001/02* (DoH)   7

Modernising Social Services (DoH)   8

Multidisciplinary assessment   71–73

Multidisciplinary teams   25, 49–52,
                    54–56,85–92;
                    Case Study 5 (p34)
                    Case Study 6A; 6B (p35; 36)
                    Case Study 10 (p59),
                    Case Study 11 (p60)

(*see also* Therapists)

Multiple pathology   18, 65

N

National Beds Inquiry   139

National Priorities Guidance   130

National Service Framework
    (NSF) for Older People   9, 129

NHS Act 1999 6,   131

Non-professional staff   109–112

North Devon Re-ablement Teams   91;
                    Case Study 6A; 6B (p35; 36)
                    Case Study 9 (p56),
                    Case Study 10 (p59), *Box F* (p94)

North West Surrey   127–128;
                    Case Study 18 (pp89-90)

North Yorkshire Pilot Social
    Rehabilitation Scheme,
    Scarborough   *Case Study 3* (p27);
                    Box F (p94)

Nottingham City Social Services
    Department   *Case Study 17* (p82);
                    Box F (p94)

Nuffield Institute for Health,
    University of Leeds   *Box B* (p29)

Nursing homes   3, 72

Nursing roles   29–30; *Box A* (p16)
    community rehabilitation   52

O

Oaks Resource Centre, Bradford   57;
                    Case Study 7 (p38)

Occupational therapy
    accident and emergency
        units   *Case Study 15* (p80)
    community rehabilitation   32, 82;
                    Case Study 16 (p81)
                    Case Study 17 (p82)
    initial contacts   98
    inpatient rehabilitation   28–30
    non-professional assistants   109–111
    role of therapists   Appendix 3
    social rehabilitation schemes   45–46
    staffing levels   101–105
    stroke units   32

Organisation of services   14, 21–25,
                    65–66, 97
    stroke care   93–97
    team work   25, 49–52, 54–56, 85–92,
                    Case Study 5 (p34)
                    Case Study 6A (p35)
                    Case Study 9 (p56),
                    Case Study 10 (p59),
                    Case Study 11 (p60)

Outlands, Plymouth   *Case Study 1A, 1B*
                    (pp23, 24)

Outreach services   82

Overtime   105

P

Partnership for Improvement
    (Welsh Office)   6, 131

Partnership in Action (DoH)   6, 131

Patient involvement   74–76

Physiotherapy
    community rehabilitation   52
    initial contacts   98
    inpatient rehabilitation   28–30
    input units   *Box E* (p67);
                    Case Study 12 (p67)
    non-professional assistants   109;
                    Case Study 13 (p78)
    role of therapists   Appendix 3
    social rehabilitation schemes   45–46
    staffing levels   101–105
    stroke units   32

Plymouth Social Services
    Department   *Case Study 1A, 1B*
                    (pp23, 24)

Princess Royal Hospital,
    Haywards Heath   *Case Study 15* (p80);
                    Box F (p94)

Protocols   82

Q

Qualified staff therapy time
    contribution to recovery   108–109
    inpatient rehabilitation   28–31
    social rehabilitation schemes   45–46
    stroke units   32

R

Re-ablement model   55–57;
                    Case Study 6A; 6B (pp35, 36)

Rehabilitation
    access   12, 51
    alternatives to hospital or
        residential care   3–5
    care pathways
        assessment   13, 71–73;
                    Case Study 8 (p48);
                    Box C (p50)
        care planning   74–76
        continuity of care   15, 77–84
        screening   68–70
    definition   6–10
    effectiveness   11
    nurse's role   29–30; *Box A* (p16)
    organisation   14, 21–25, 65–66, 97
        stroke care   93–97
        team work   21–25, 49, 54–56,
                    Case Study 5 (p34)
                    Case Study 6A; 6B (pp35, 36)
    provision of services
        see Service provision
    special needs of older
        people 1   6–24, 65–66
        strategic approach   118–120
            cost-effectiveness   134–140;
                    Box F (p94)
            financial flexibility   131–133
        shared understanding
            between health and social
            services   120–122
        whole systems approach 126–128;
                    Case study 18 (p89–90)
    therapists *see* Therapists

Residential care
    social services residential
        rehabilitation schemes   38–47;
                Case Study 1A; 1B, (pp23, 24)
                    Case Study 2 (p26)
                    Case Study 3 (p27);
    unnecessary admissions   3, 72–73

Rotherham Community
    Assessment Rehabilitation
    and Treatment Scheme
                Case Study 4 (p33)

Rotherham Residential
    Rehabilitation Scheme   *Case Study 2*
               (p26); *Box F* (p94)

Royal College of Nursing   30;
                    Box C (p50)

Royal College of Physicians   9, 29

S

Scarborough, North Yorkshire
    Pilot Social Rehabilitation
    Scheme   *Case Study 3* (p27);
                    Box F (p94)

Screening   68–70

Service provision   26
    day and community-based
        services   24–25, 48–57, 81;
                    Case Study 4 (p33)
                    Case Study 5 (p34)
            Case Study 6A; 6B (pp35, 36)
                    Case Study 7 (p38)
    inpatient rehabilitation   28–31, 58
    intermediate rehabilitation
        services   24–25, 35–47
    linking services 6–15, 58–66, 126–130
    measuring availability   27–28
    stroke units   32–34

Sheffield Community Rehabilitation
    Teams   82; *Case Study 5* (p34)

Sheffield Standardised Screening
    Assessment   *Case Study 8* (p48)

Skill mix   108–110

Social services departments   123

Social services residential
    rehabilitation schemes   38–47;
             Case Study 1A; 1B, (pp23, 24)
                    Case Study 2 (p26)
                    Case Study 3 (p27)

Speech and language therapy
    community rehabilitation   52
    initial contacts   98
    inpatient rehabilitation   29–31

role of therapists   Appendix 3
staffing levels   101–104
stroke units   32

St Richards Hospital, Chichester   111;
             Case Study 13 (p78)

Staff time
    contribution to recovery   108–109
    inpatient rehabilitation   28–31
    social rehabilitation schemes   45–46
    stroke units   32

Staffing levels   101–107
    flexible deployment   113–117
    non-professional assistants   109–112

Stockport Hospital NHS Trust   100

Strategic planning   118–119
    cost-effectiveness of
        rehabilitation   134–140
    financial flexibility   131–133
    shared understanding between
        health and social services   120–122
    whole-systems approach   126–128,
                Case Study 18 (pp89–90)

Stroke Association   94

Stroke Unit Trialists Collaboration   21,
                93; *Box F* (p94)

Stroke units   32–34, 93–97
    Bradford   92; *Case Study 11* (p60)

Strokes   2, 19–22, 69–70
    continuity of care   79–80
    equipment at home   80
    explanation to patients   74–76
    impact of strokes   Appendix 2
    organisation and delivery
        of care   94–97
    stroke user survey   Appendix 2

T

Team work   21–25, 49, 54–56;
                  Case Study 5 (p34)
        Case Study 6A; 6B (pp35, 36)

Therapists
    calculating inputs   Appendix 3
    flexibility   113–117
    maximising use of skills   108–112;
                  Case Study 13 (p78)
                  Case Study 14 (p79)
    measuring demand   99–104
    national shortages   102–107
    non-professional assistants   109–112
    roles   Appendix 3
    service levels   101

Therapy time
    contribution to recovery   108–109
    inpatient rehabilitation   28–31
    social rehabilitation schemes   45–46
    stroke units   32

Time management   *see* Therapy time

Trends in Rehabilitation Policy
    (Audit Commission and
    King's Fund)   10

U

United They Stand
    (Audit Commission)   3

University of Leeds   *Box B* (p29)

Universtiy of Sheffield   52; *Box C* (p50)

University of York   *Box B* (p29),
                    Box F (p94)

University of York Health
    Economics Consortium   43;
                  Case Study 2 (p26)
                  Case Study 4 (p33)

V

Victoria Project, London   *Case Study 16*
             (p81); *Box F* (p94)

W

West Sussex, Princess
    Royal Hospital   *Case Study 15* (p80);
                    Box F (p94)

Westminster Social Services
                Case Study 16 (p81)

Whole systems approach   126–128;
             Case Study 18 (pp89–90)

World Health Organisation
             Appendix 2, Part A